PRACTICAL SUGGESTIONS FOR TEACHING

edited by ALICE MIEL

Social Studies for Understanding

Titles in This Series

Social Studies

for

Understanding

BY

HELEN FISHER DARROW

BUREAU OF PUBLICATIONS

TEACHERS COLLEGE, COLUMBIA UNIVERSITY

NEW YORK • 1964

EDITOR'S FOREWORD

HELEN FISHER DARROW HAS INVESTED YEARS IN THINKING THROUGH and discussing with others ways social studies teaching may be improved. She has worked with many teachers to help them develop more confidence in their ability to make important decisions about the social studies program in their own classrooms. In return, these teacher colleagues of Dr. Darrow have generously shared descriptions of social studies teaching which went beyond the ordinary for them.

The author, then, has brought to this writing her firm conviction that social studies can and must make a difference in children's lives. She has explained clearly how a teacher may take the difficult step of choosing to deal with fresh and important information about people. And she has given countless examples of actual classroom work to illuminate the points made.

This booklet, Dr. Darrow's second contribution to this series, is designed to help teachers conduct useful, meaningful, life-related unit studies, drawing substantial content from various disciplines. The author hopes that teachers will help children understand how life is really lived by people around the globe, care about others and themselves, and take socially useful action. Developments in all parts of our nation and world indicate a great urgency for social studies to give just such help to our children.

ALICE MIEL

CONTENTS

Social Studies

for

Understanding

Chapter I

A DIRECTION FOR SOCIAL STUDIES

To THE TEACHER WHO WISHES TO THINK THROUGH HIS SOCIAL STUDIES program, the task can seem very baffling. Making choices is seldom easy, but making choices in social studies teaching is especially difficult, for in this area a teacher faces a multitude of possibilities from which to choose.

There are *goals* to decide upon in the face of formidable lists of desirable ones: "What goals," asks the thoughtful teacher, *"should* I select?"

There is *content* to choose, and the scope of possible content to study seems almost endless. The teacher now asks, "What content *should* I choose?"

There are class *procedures* to select from a kaleidoscopic array. "What procedures," the teacher asks, *"should* I follow?"

There are *materials* to consider and their number and variety are increasing rapidly. "What materials," queries the teacher once more, *"should* I consider?"

As though such choice-making were not difficult enough, the situation is made more bewildering by the intangible quality of social studies. Here is an area of study whose shape must continually be defined to a large degree in terms of shifting social emphases and impact. Arithmetic and science do not present this difficulty. They offer a relative amount of concreteness and, consequently, recent proposals for new shapes in these areas have had the advantage of being rather easily communicated and adopted.

Not so social studies. Its elusive nature has discouraged attempts to reshape it. Yet reshaping is necessary if social studies is to be tailored to the changing times and urgent demands for social prog-

1

ress. The gap between the present curriculum structure and pressing social realities only leaves the teacher in a bigger muddle than ever.

It is no wonder, then, that teachers sometimes resort to aimless content and procedures. The teacher who explains his unit-study on freight trains in terms of a district requirement; the teacher who views social studies mainly as an opportunity for activity projects in art and construction; the teacher who justifies social studies as fact-collecting experiences; the teacher who thinks of social studies only in terms of group "citizenship" experiences; the teacher who emphasizes, not people, but things like boats, weapons, or crops; the teacher who thinks of social studies in terms of covering a textbook—these are teachers who understandably may have become confused about the direction for social studies.

When taught by instructors like these, social studies turns out to be a disappointing field, and there is little hope of its values being realized in children's thinking and behavior. Yet no area of the elementary school curriculum holds more promise than social studies for fulfilling man's tremendous need for *understanding* his fellow man and *acting* constructively to solve his basic problems of human interaction.

To clear the way toward a new, revitalized social studies for today it seems appropriate to ask, What goes wrong with social studies?

What Goes Wrong with Social Studies?

The purposes which might be achieved through social studies have not been accomplished to an appreciable extent. Why?

FRAMEWORKS

Most frameworks or guides to social studies content fail to build upon important bases of social studies—society's deep values, children's ways of learning, and the social realities of the times. While many introductions to frameworks recognize these bases, the frameworks themselves usually show little relationship to the introductions. As the contents of study areas and topics are spelled out, frameworks ignore their introductions and organize subject matter within standard geographical–historical boundaries.

Children understand their world as they have contact with it, directly and indirectly. The world in terms of city-county-state space lines and month-year-century time lines means little to them.[1] To insist upon using such space-time lines for frameworks only encourages repetition of content, with slight variations each year. For example, study one year of the neighborhood grocery store leads to studies the following years of community food production, then state, national, and finally hemispheric food production. These divisions have little to do with the significant realities of social living. Without sound bases consistently implemented, frameworks can give no true direction for teaching and, therefore, no foundation for planning studies. No wonder, then, that frameworks as they now exist too often limit the vision of both teachers and children who might otherwise reach out to embrace the impinging environment; who might otherwise seek studies in harmony with the fundamental bases of social studies. Like architectural designs not built for the people who must use them, frameworks too easily become nonfunctional. When used to do teachers' and children's thinking for them, the result is particularly sad. Teachers must look beyond even the best framework, far beyond it indeed, to discover vital purposes for social studies. They must search more deeply for ways to build significant unit-studies.

ACTIVITIES

Activities undertaken for show and "something to do" deny the nature of social studies. As a curriculum area incorporating several related fields of knowledge, social studies rests on certain basic ideas which, if understood and accepted as values, become triggers to individual and group action. Understanding is necessary if action is to be intelligent. Without understanding, action too easily becomes pointless and meaningless—a blind, unreasoned adventure. This does not mean that activity is not necessary; it is, of course, a necessary part of learning. When used deliberately to build un-

[1]See Frank Estvan and Elizabeth Estvan, *The Child's World; His Social Perception* (New York: G. P. Putnam's Sons, 1959), Chapter 23.

derstandings and fulfill them in action, activity has a strong purpose. But always activities must be used deliberately and carefully to keep the stress upon understanding. The desired understandings, not the activities, must be the reason for organizing unit-studies. Otherwise, while there may be periods when children are temporarily absorbed in activities, social studies is a dead-end street.

FACTS

Facts do not make ideas, although they are part of them. Facts mean little in themselves and give no direction for organizing social studies. When they are sorted out, however, according to the understandings to be achieved, they do provide the details by means of which big ideas are understood. Related to understandings, facts become meaningful and useful. Unrelated, facts fall flat—as does social studies.

SUBJECTS

As threads placed side by side never make cloth, so subjects taught side by side do not add up to social studies. Only as they are interwoven to form social understandings useful in dealing with life do subjects function as social studies. Social understandings—the big ideas of social studies—belong to many subjects: history, geography, philosophy, political science, anthropology, economics, psychology, sociology; and to many branches of these: industrial, social, economic, and physical geography; or archeological, linguistic, ethnological, and cultural anthropology. In the world of action, these subjects are merged and often lose their separate identities. Who is to say whether public finance is economics or political science; whether religion belongs to philosophy, psychology, sociology, or history? And what about international relations or public opinion? Even history does not speak with one voice, but is political or social or economic according to its use.

Of course ideas relating to a specific subject deserve correct terminology whenever they are used, even with young children. There are times, too, when certain children need to delve into a particular social science. In fact, certain individuals have begun to urge that children learn the "structure of a discipline" and experience a scholar's approach to subject matter. By so doing, they say, children will better grasp the key concepts of fields such as history, geography, and anthropology.[2]

But every child has the right to be helped first and foremost to gain understanding of his social world—as he encounters it, not as scholars have organized it for purposes of their own further research. The organization of studies should recognize clearly and directly a child's right to understand his world through a problem or goal-centered approach.

PEOPLE

Understandings about the world which fail to focus upon people deny the core of social studies—people and their human interactions. People are alive and changing. They have pasts which affect their present and future; they have personal and impersonal relationships, close and far away.

Without people for study there are no social studies. What people think and why, what they believe and do, their problems—these must be in the spotlight for study. Whenever the spotlight turns to other animals, nature's way and products or even the "thing" aspects of man's inventions without reference to their impact on man, social studies gives way to other study areas. Learning the names of boats and ships, the causes of desert and jungle, the mechanical process of pasteurization or gardening or flying an airplane—these subjects belong to the world of study perhaps, but not the world of social studies. Social studies should unremittingly focus upon the human elements of living.

SOCIAL LEARNINGS

Social learnings are the hoped-for outcomes of social studies. They come in the form of social understandings, feelings, and skills. They may be promoted throughout the school day as teachers and pupils plan and evaluate together; as they learn to value one another; and as children have chances to communicate with one an-

2See Alice Miel, "Knowledge and the Curriculum," in Alexander Frazier (Ed.), *New Insights and the Curriculum: Yearbook 1963* (Washington, D.C.: Association for Supervision and Curriculum Development, 1963), Chapter 4.

other, to work together, and relate to one another, whatever the area of study. However, many valuable opportunities for developing social learnings are lost unless there is a strong social studies offering, carefully designed to develop significant social understandings and to help individuals and groups move to responsible action.

When children pursue social studies, they go to one or more sources of information in an organized search for knowledge on a topic or a problem. Thus, many socially oriented projects and experiences may be turned into social studies concerns. For example, preparation of a class newspaper can move to a study of the role of print in people's lives; a toothbrush sale underwritten by the local P–TA, to a study of the purposes of the P–TA and other voluntary organizations in a democracy. Opportunities like these help children to integrate their feelings and thoughts, so that their thinking is both informed and buttressed by compassion and empathy. When feelings and thoughts are left separated, learning too remains on a superficial, restricted level. In studies which emphasize both feeling and thought as one, children will be able to experience the deepest kind of learning to be had—the discovery and rediscovery of both personal meanings and social values. In this way social studies opens the way to social learnings. To correct the misconceptions about social studies and the consequent failure of social studies to promote social learnings (which it has the potential for doing), the direction for social studies should be re-examined.

New Direction for Social Studies

When goals are clearly and simply stated in terms of desired behavior, social studies can be used to develop understandings *directly related* to the goals. By opening direct lines from goals to related understandings it is possible to make choices of pertinent content for study and experience. Thus the clutter of preselected unit titles and study areas, which have no functional relationship with the hoped-for behavioral outcomes, can be eliminated.

The hoped-for outcomes arise within the many areas of human

interaction and challenge. People face every day the challenges of such interactions as identifying with other people, governing themselves, communicating with others, participating in work, choosing goods and services, using time, and getting an education. Only as they learn to understand the demands of living can people work actively and intelligently to make choices in harmony with social values. Only as they become aware of the conflicts and alternatives open for action can people strengthen their beliefs and work to make needed changes in the social world.

Teachers who become thoroughly familiar with areas of human interaction put themselves in a strategic position to plan social studies for classroom action. Reflection on the significance of these areas will suggest outcomes to work for and give implications for teaching.

AREAS OF INTERACTION AND CHALLENGE

While there are many ways to analyze the areas of interaction, a brief examination here of some of the areas represents an attempt to view them in relation to goals for social studies teaching.[3]

Identifying with people of the world and their problems. Close living, whether as nations or as individuals, brings many problems, among them the paradoxical need to maintain privacy, for inner satisfaction, while building a sense of relatedness to others through friendships and empathies. How well the individual does this depends largely upon his understanding and acceptance of himself as a person.

Individuals who see themselves as capable of solving their own problems and winning respect from others tend to have the ability to accept other people's problems as also worthy of attention, and the energy to help in their solution. The individual, himself a product of a particular culture and certain cohesive groups, has to learn to see himself in relation to his culture and group memberships, as well as in comparison with individuals in other cultures and other groups.

[3]Office of the Superintendent of Schools, San Diego County, Calif., *Social Studies—Grades One Through Eight* (A course of study prepared by a committee of six: William Abbott, Clifford Hatch, Edwena Moore, DeGrof Platte, Ralph Taylor, and Helen Fisher Darrow, 1958).

Consequently, it is expected that the person educated to the need of identifying with people and their problems will:

be comfortable with himself;
be sensitive to resources available to help solve his problems;
accept the problems of others as being real and worthy of concern;
work to reduce barriers between people.

In this connection social studies can become a deliberate means, whatever the grade, for deepening understanding of the need to improve the quality of individual and group relationships. It can become a way to help children of all grades to gain insights into personal and group problems which will enable them to identify more easily with people of the world and their problems.

Governing ourselves in a democratic society. In our society decision-making rightfully belongs to the individual, who is believed to be the best judge of what is good for him. A democratic society affirms, too, that individuals can work together voluntarily to solve their problems and arrive at common agreements. As decisions affect larger numbers of people, however, some decisions concerning the individual must be made without his direct participation. Thus there is always a pull and push on the individual. He must ever guard his rights to self-government, yet must accept group limits to his action in the best interests of all.

Since the individual is part of government, he must learn to see himself as a citizen responsible for working in the public sphere to improve the process of government designed to carry out its citizens' wishes. Fundamental to this is the learning of self-control, the kind which means, first, integrating oneself around a core of values and, second, taking responsibility for self-made decisions.

Consequently, it is expected that the person educated to the need for governing himself in a democratic society will:

be committed to a value system based upon individual worth and
    dignity;
be committed to a belief that men working together can solve their own
    problems;
live within the boundaries to individual action set by group regulations;
work for necessary change in govermental form and structure.

Social studies can become a deliberate means—whatever the grade—for deepening understanding of the need to improve the quality of decision-making on all levels of government. It can become a way to help children of all ages gain insights into their own role in decision-making which will enable them to govern themselves better in a democratic society.

Communicating with others in a free world. Messages get to people in a number of ways: through face-to-face contacts with free exchange; through larger group meetings with more restricted exchange; through mass media with highly limited exchange; and through words, thoughts, feelings, and gestures. It takes effort to understand the viewpoints of others and to extend one's own viewpoints accurately. Individuals who themselves think clearly and deeply are likely to be better able to judge critically what others say and to guard against uniformity in thinking.

Because our society values freedom of speech and thought, the individual must assume responsibility to distinguish between fact and opinion, truth and fallacy, open and closed conclusions. As he learns to see himself as a thinking, speaking individual capable of maintaining personal integrity in the use of language, he becomes better able to recognize the open exchange of ideas as essential to democratic progress.

Consequently, it is expected that the person educated to the need for communicating with others in a free world will:

assume responsibility for making himself understood;
strive to understand the viewpoints of others and the reasons for them;
withhold judgment until available facts are gathered;
work to increase the free flow of information.

Social studies can become a means—whatever the grade—for deepening understanding of the need to improve the quality of shared ideas and information, thoughts, and feelings. It can become a way to help children gain insights into the consequences of words which will enable them to communicate with others in a free world.

Participating in the world of work. Today, as in the days of the Puritans, work is an honored and necessary feature of living. In spite of changes in work demands and conditions, workers themselves are still the resource without which no country progresses. For the well-being of both the individual and the nation, manpower resources require careful planning and development.

Work which interests and challenges the worker also gives him the necessary energy for fulfilling the demands of production. The worker's own life becomes enriched when he chooses work well-suited to him and finds stimulating conditions in which to work. Yet he must anticipate and plan for job shifts as some work demands diminish and other possibilities open up. Airplane workers may need to learn to convert to missile industries, typesetters to electronic tape operators. The individual who has learned to recognize his potentialities and maintain himself in varied work patterns will be best able to accept himself as a productive worker.

Consequently, it is expected that the person educated to the need to participate in the world of work will:

maintain himself as a self-supporting and contributing member of society;

choose his occupation in line with his interests and abilities and in terms of the possibilities open to him;

be sensitive to the contributions of organizations and individuals in promoting economic well-being;

be able to adapt to changing work demands.

Social studies can become a means—whatever the grade—for deepening understanding of the need to improve the quality of workmanship and working conditions. It can become a way to help children gain insights into their own potentialities and conditions for productive work which will enable them to participate eagerly in the world of work.

Making use of time. Time can be man's powerful resource or his severe limitation, depending upon how he chooses to use it. With industries moving toward reducing working hours, with automatic devices employed increasingly in the home and the shop, the individual finds more time free from labor demands. This time may be frittered away by rushing endlessly about on trivial errands or by settling down before the television set. It may be used, on the other hand, to pursue satisfying hobbies, or engage in creative activities, reflective thinking, or sports.

Choices can be made which will promote both personal and group satisfactions, if the individual plans his time to allow for work with voluntary services and community problems, as well as personal interests. Individuals who have experienced satisfactions in their own use of time should work more vigorously to provide facilities and improve conditions which will make it possible for others also to pursue time in rewarding ways.

Consequently, it is expected that the person educated to the need of making fruitful use of time will:

have a wide variety of interests and skills;
recognize a responsibility to keep himself physically, mentally, and emotionally sound;
assume a social responsibility for constructive use of time in the community.

Social studies can become a means—whatever the grade—for deepening understanding of the need to use time productively. It can become a way to help children of all ages to gain insights into the factors affecting their use of time which will enable them to assume more responsibility in making use of time.

Choosing and using goods and services. Money plays an important, though limited, role in the American way of life, giving unprecedented opportunities to live comfortably. However, each consumer has the continuing problem of selecting those goods and services which best suit his purposes, and each community, state, and nation has the problem of making goods and services available. Both public and private choices need to recognize long-term goals as well as immediately satisfying ones. With the resources of the world unequally distributed, the need arises to maintain careful use, conservation, and replenishment of the world's resources for the benefit of all. New resources and improved uses of those already available must be sought continuously. The individual who learns to see himself as a consumer in relation to all other consumers should be able also to feel concern for the economic welfare and progress of all peoples.

Consequently, it is expected that the person educated to the need for choosing and using goods and services wisely will:

weigh possible choices in terms of both personal satisfaction and group welfare;

make long-term plans for the use and conservation of his resources;

share responsibility for conserving and developing the resources of the world;

make effective use of his money for maximum benefit to himself and others.

Social studies can become a means—whatever the grade—for deepening understanding of the need to improve the quality of consumership. It can become a way to help children of all ages to gain insight into their own problems as consumers and to choose and use more wisely the goods and services for both personal and general welfare.

Getting an education. Education is more than schooling; it is a lifelong process for individuals who are eager to learn. At the same time that education serves to stimulate individual growth, it is used to perpetuate a group's culture and beliefs among young and old. Every society depends upon education for its survival and progress. In our society, public schools are charged both with inculcating the democratic way of life and loyalty to democracy's values, and with stimulating individual potentiality.

Consequently, it is expected that the person educated to the need for getting an education will:

maintain an eagerness for learning;

develop responsibility for continuing his education beyond compulsory limits;

maintain faith in public education;

work to improve the educational program.

Social studies can become a means—whatever the grade—for deepening understanding of the need to raise the level of education for all. It can become a way to help children gain insights into the powers of a democratic education which will enable them throughout their lives to get education for personal and group fulfillment.

USE OF SIGNIFICANT UNDERSTANDINGS

Within all these areas of experience, social studies can be used to help children live more intelligently and responsibly if the program develops the high-quality understandings which the behavioral outcomes to be achieved demand. Understandings which show only on paper-and-pencil tests will not do. It takes the kind which penetrate deep into the nervous system and which result in action; the kind of understandings which move a citizen to oppose vigorously such lawlessness as lynching, to work for slum clearance, to fight for a free press, to be on the lookout for fire hazards, to campaign for a recreational park to be used by all.

Understandings cannot, unfortunately, be instilled in an individual once and for all, to be fixed for all time. They must grow with experience and study over the years. With understandings as direction for teaching, however, teachers can plan particular studies which will open up or extend awareness.

Through a study of peer relationships, for illustration, a teacher might deliberately seek to build awareness of the need to understand and accept oneself as a worth-while person. The pupil could be led to recognize that we are unable to relate to all people in a like manner, and that how we see ourselves depends upon how we think others see us.

Through a study of people's prejudices or a survey of holiday customs or perhaps a comparison of rural life in the United States and elsewhere, a teacher, irrespective of grade, might seek to build awareness of the need to value likenesses and differences among people. Many differences in people come from the culture in which they live and the personal values they hold. People living together may hold different values within a common framework. These understandings serve as stabilizers in setting the focus for social studies planning. Deeper and broader than any particular topic for study, the same set of understandings can be used by teachers of all grade levels and developed through any number of topics. Kindergarten is not too soon to begin.

Topic titles are not sacred; to be reserved for a special year of life. Whether some individuals once studied the vikings in the fourth grade, others the ancient Greeks, and still others the state in which they lived at the time seems to make little difference in adult demonstration of outcomes. Demonstration of the desired outcomes depends, not upon a particular title, but upon the understandings gained. This does not mean that any study selected is as promising as another for yielding understandings, or that a certain study developed in any fashion yields equal results. Both the particular selection and the development of a study make a vital difference, as later chapters suggest. Younger children handle topics within their interest and grasp; older children respond to those within their interests and abilities. But always the emphasis remains upon understanding. For only in this way can social studies vigorously, persistently, and directly contribute to the hoped-for outcomes of thought and action.

Chapter II

MAKING CHOICES OF STUDIES

PLACEMENT OF RESPONSIBILITY FOR CHOICE OF TOPICS OR PROBLEMS to be pursued varies of course among school districts. But teachers usually have some degree of freedom in making their choice, whether or not they choose to exercise this freedom. Mrs. W. describes her experience in this way:

I mentioned to my principal that I would like to think through my own group study instead of following the state framework. He agreed. So I turned to an understanding—that people working together can solve their own problems. I was not sure how to develop it, but in the month since the school began, I sensed a need among my group to realize and handle this understanding with perception and skill.

I tried to launch a study of human problems and how they had been solved. It fell flat; the group showed neither a grasp nor interest. I looked for another route. The opportunity came—election of officers in the class and coincidentally of community officials. The matter of leadership emerged as a natural study idea and one which could give sharp focus to the understanding I had in mind.

Another group of children might not have responded to the stirrings of election campaigns. A different teacher might have found it more urgent to work toward some other understanding. In any case, when the first idea for a study did not "take," the teacher dropped it without feeling a sense of personal failure. By showing confidence in children's intelligence and in her own skill as a teacher, she avoided the interpersonal stresses and strains caused by forcing a study. This did not mean that she was merely following the path of least resistance. There were sound bases for the choices she made.

Using Criteria for Study Selection

Any teacher is more likely to have confidence in his ability to select appropriate content when he has carefully stated criteria to guide him.

CRITERION ONE: CONTRIBUTION TO UNDERSTANDING

Because any content selected for classroom study must be aimed directly at the understandings needed for intelligent, democratic behavior, the understandings themselves suggest giving priority to certain content.

Some understandings are as all-encompassing as this sampling of themes proposed by the National Commission on Social Studies in its report:[1]

Recognition and understanding of world *interdependence.*
Recognition of the *dignity and worth of the individual.*
Use of *intelligence* to improve human living.
Responsibility for achieving social action.
Cooperation in the interest of peace and welfare.
Achieving a balance between *social stability and social change.*

It is possible to work directly from such a broad theme to build the content of a study, as in this teacher's experience:

I chose to concentrate on the reality of change as a major understanding and looked about for a topic of interest to the children. With astronauts so much in their conversations, I opened a discussion of man's travel to the moon. The group responded excitedly and talked at length about spaceship travel. We made plans for an organized study.

Another teacher stressed the same theme through a study of old and new ways of living, the group comparing households and schools then, that is before grandmother's time, and now. A third teacher also used the theme of change in developing a study of man's explorations into the unknown through the fields of medicine, land-sea discoveries, and space conquests—three areas which the group selected for intensive study.

[1]National Council for the Social Studies, *A Guide to Content in the Social Studies: Report of the NCSS Committees on Concepts and Values* (National Education Association, Washington, D.C., 1958), pp. 6 ff.

Within each area of human challenge represented by the broad themes discussed in Chapter I it is possible to state a somewhat clearer goal of understanding along with a set of related understandings. For example, within the area of Choosing and Using Goods and Services, one goal of understanding might be "Realize the importance of using human resources wisely."[2] From this can be drawn these related understandings:

that society needs to provide opportunity for all its members to make their greatest possible contribution;
that efforts must be made to utilize fully the special abilities of such groups as the gifted, handicapped, aged, and retired;
that intelligent solutions must be found for the problems which create war, disease, poverty, and mental–emotional instability.

Working toward the identical understanding, one teacher helped a group of children concentrate near the Christmas season on problems of practicing safety at home; another helped children of the same age to work near the summer vacation time on questions of camping and picnicking, with emphasis on why people take time for rest and recreation. An older group, found to be indifferent to one another's contributions, spent time surveying members' talents and expertness to prepare a "resource file" for class and school use. The group also studied the need for specialists and experts in solving modern problems and became acquainted with world leaders who were famous for their contributions to mankind.

Goals of understanding may take the form also of specific understandings related to larger understandings, yet drawn from particular study content. The various levels of goals of understanding fit together in a fashion shown in Chart A on pages 18 and 19.

However they are expressed, understandings provide the teacher with a guide for evaluating the pertinence of content to be selected. Many understandings emerge during study as children make their own discoveries and arrive at their own personal interpretations from the materials studied. But with a major understanding or two clearly in mind, the teacher has a direction for working, without sacrificing flexibility in choice of content.

[2]Office of the Superintendent of Schools, San Diego County, *Social Studies, Grades One through Eight,* 1958, p. 32.

CHART A

Two Illustrations of Levels of Understanding

	Key
A study in the area of "Getting an Education,"	Area of interaction
emphasizing the theme of "intelligence,"	Theme
focused upon the goal of understanding: *to understand the ways the individual gets his education,* which includes: understanding that education goes on throughout life, understanding that there are many ways for individuals to learn in addition to those ways provided by schools,	Related understandings: General
using the study topic, "Organizing a Class Library,"	Topic for study
with the specific understanding, *libraries help us learn.*	Related understandings: Specific

Key

A study in the area of "Participating in the World of Work,"			Area of interaction
	emphasizing the theme of "interdependence,"		Theme
		focused upon the goal of understanding:	Related understandings:
		to realize how scientific knowledge and techniques change ways people work and live, which includes:	
			General
		understanding that technological advances create new problems as well as new opportunities in patterns of work and living,	
		using the study topic, "The Motel Business,"	Topic for study
		with specific understandings:	Related understandings:
		motels are a growing business to meet demands for overnight facilities;	Specific
		older and smaller hotels and motels have problems of competing with large-chain and new motels for customer business.	

With no goal of understanding in mind, the danger of going down a blind alley increases, as in this case.

I prepared a firsthand experience in butter-making which was listed as an activity in the dairy unit. We bought ingredients, procured a churn and spent an hour or so having children take turns churning butter. We left some butter unsalted. Children tasted both. Then we wrote a chart story, pointing up the difference between salted and unsalted butter.

Had the teacher selected the information and activity with significant goals of understanding in mind, perhaps the understanding of change, she might have used the same butter-making activity to draw attention to the contrast of modern and outmoded methods, not to concentrate upon the flavor of butter. In selecting content, the teacher has this question to answer: How directly will this study help these children to achieve some of the understandings so essential to democratic living? By using the criterion of contribution to understanding, the teacher has a primary point of reference.

CRITERION TWO: RELATIONSHIP TO CONTEMPORARY
    AFFAIRS AND SOCIAL REALITIES

Because children must themselves meet the challenge of modern living, the use of realistic, persistent, and contemporary content gives the teacher a second criterion for selection—relationship to contemporary affairs and social realities. Realistic content for thinking emerges when children deal with such live issues as planning leisure or getting people out to vote.

In our democracy, where problems must be solved by the people themselves, failure to adapt to the real dimensions of social affairs and conditions may mean failure to gain insights needed for problem-solving. The problems of war and peace, freedom and security, economic stability and well-being, racial and intergroup relations, population stresses, limited resources and unlimited needs and desires all persist today as in past centuries. These problems call for solution in their current forms.

Within their levels of understanding and interest, children need countless opportunities to analyze controversial issues and apply critical thinking to problems and affairs at hand. There is no suggestion here that history be ignored. The persistence of unsolved problems makes it necessary for people to use historical perspective to gain a better grasp of contemporary problems. But such instruction does not depend upon following a logical or chronological order when the direction is that of increased understanding, and the emphasis is upon social realities. Children confront social realities when they become aware of life as it is actually lived and when they work with realistic content. Unrealistic attitudes like these have no place in classroom content:

Mothers and fathers are unselfish people who think only of their children.

Community helpers—the policeman, postman, and fireman—perform their duties merely for the sake of serving others.

American heroes were perfect, flawless gentlemen.

Children may be misled in other ways also. Those who continue to be taught, for example, that there is room for only one "best" and everyone must compete for this distinction, learn to ignore the newer realities of intra-team and inter-team cooperation. They do not have an opportunity to learn that individuals and teams can work together to build rules and standards of conduct and that individual rivalry works against productiveness.

Children who learn that the individual, and especially certain individuals, counts for little, have no perspective for learning that democratic living is a reality, not a dream.

Children who learn that the individual, and especially certain peoples of the Western world or hemisphere cannot learn that East and West now meet. Giving the bakery, dairy, and market priority over other goods and services suggests unrealistic emphasis in an age where all kinds of goods have become essentials—from frozen foods to plastics and laundromats. Choices of content which children can accept as important and which, at the same time, touch many people in timely fashion are generally found not in textbooks but in the daily environment. Alert teachers will find innumerable clues in current events. Weekly and monthly news magazines followed regularly over a period of time reveal possible leads ranging from new businesses like the greeting card industry to new problems like food storage to new advancements like the future of cultural institutions to new conquests like the boom of roadbuilding. Newspapers constantly report national and local events as well as special drives. School affairs often create problems very real to children, yet related to larger questions of social significance, as in this case reported by a teacher.

The mayor's daughter left school as a result of scandal touching several city officials. While perhaps not entirely understanding the meanings of graft, corruption, and extortion, the children were acutely aware of the absence of other classmates as the circle of accusation among families spread. The problem of teaching the practices and principles of democratic government and safeguards against its malfunction had become a personal one involving not remote politicians but our neighbors.

Some realities take precedence over others, of course, as they relate more closely to the outcomes desired and the goals of understanding to be achieved. In selecting appropriate content the teacher has to answer the question, To what extent will this content allow for experience in real problem-solving and critical thinking, as well as the pursuit of questions meaningful to children, yet related to larger public issues?

By using the criterion of relationship to contemporary affairs and social realities, the teacher earns a second point of reference.

If we accept thinking as a basic function of the schools, there can be no escape from giving children genuine experiences in making decisions regarding study content. Decisions cannot be made without considering children's interests whether already developed or newly stimulated, for interests are an integral part of decision-making. Thus what children are, or become, interested in forms a third criterion to use in content selection.

CRITERION THREE: RELATIONSHIP TO CHILDREN'S CURIOSITIES AND RESPONSES

Children's curiosities include a variety of topics and questions about man's discoveries, explorations, development, and past existence. They include questions about distant peoples, and queries related to their own immediate surroundings. Children become curious about the people they meet through either direct contact or indirect contact. Viewing on television a queen's coronation or a dramatization of a great American's biography; reading a story of ancient Egyptian life; visiting Old Ironsides or the Alamo; these events may stimulate more personalized reflections than does daily contact with the milkman or postman. The key is what has personal meaning for the child. Curiosities which take on personal meaning become potential material for study.

Alert teachers probe both apparent and latent interests to discover leads for study. At times the lead is a clear one.

In an assembly program we had a Navajo Indian lecturer and dancer. He explained the deep spiritual significances of some of his people's customs. When we returned to the classroom, Tom asked, "Does the good always win?" I was caught off guard, not knowing what he meant. But other children did not let the question drop; all kinds of opinions were expressed. Jim said, "Look what we did to the Indians; they were here first and we took their land." This led to other questions: How could we have driven off the Indians? What has happened to them?

Here the teacher saw clearly an opportunity, at the same time that children followed their curiosities, to combine a significant idea with realistic meaning—understanding the place of the individual in a democracy with certain related understandings:

that the exercise of individual rights carries obligation for responsible citizenship;
that individuals need to use their intelligence and resources to solve personal and group problems.

and certain specific understandings:

there are many levels of "good" and viewpoints from which to approach it;
there are conflicts of "good" which need to be resolved;
people must work to improve opportunities for "good" to win;
mistakes can often be corrected.

Sometimes there are several leads, any of which could be picked up for further study.

Teddy came into the room tugging a big box. "For Show and Tell Time," he said. His parents had been to Puerto Rico for a vacation and had brought him back some things made of rubber—a play boat, a house, and a man. We handled the objects and talked about them.

Someone asked where they got the rubber; others offered their opinions. One child asked why the people had houses like that; again reasons were conjectured. Someone else wanted to know what the children there used for play. I asked the children if they knew where Puerto Rico was.

In this instance no one topic was pursued sufficiently for the teacher to sense the group's major curiosity or to learn how genuine it was. Going into a study of rubber processing or housing construction would be likely to emphasize a science study rather than social studies, unless care was taken to relate production to the workers and consumers involved, or to the cultural variations in group living. The choice of a science or social studies emphasis would depend, of course, upon whether scientific or social understandings were the motive for study.

Even if the group were equally interested in all the leads presented, some selection would need to be made. Not every thread of interest can be picked up or justified for group study. Whatever the choice, the teacher has final responsibility for judging its significance. Here the teacher is confronted with the question, Does the content to be selected give children experience in identifying and following through their curiosities to deeper levels of thinking? An affirmative answer gives the teacher a basis for helping children to select those interests which have best potential for a worth-while and satisfying group study.

CRITERION FOUR: APPROPRIATENESS TO CHILDREN'S
BACKGROUNDS OF EXPERIENCE AND KNOWLEDGE

Between the goals of social studies and children's levels of achievement there are many gaps. Filling in the gaps in children's awareness of the social world, in their abilities to handle social skills and democratic commitments becomes a fourth major criterion in choosing appropriate content for study. Children differ, of course, in what they know and can do; they differ in their backgrounds of experience. They come from homes where the following types of stimuli for learning have or have not been present:

parents travel widely and have many foreign friends;
parents are foreigners and maintain their foreign customs;

the family still occupies the house in which it has lived for generations;
the family frequently visits museums, concerts, historical sites;
the parents read and discuss current events and use children's questions
   for discussions.

Some children who live near the ocean or a bay may or may not
understand the fisherman's life; others who live near coal mines
may or may not understand the miner's life. Some children live in
big cities but know only a small part of the area; others live in towns
where they know most of the area. Some children's parents own
retail businesses; others work in factories or offices. Some parents
are active in labor unions or agricultural cooperatives; others in
church affairs; still others keep mostly to themselves.

Some children function as members of democratically managed
families; others are more familiar with autocratic rule or laissez-
faire conditions. Some have been overprotected, others neglected.
Some children come to school with strong prejudices toward other
groups; some with amazing skill in accepting themselves and others.
Some come well-informed about the world of work, but not about
using leisure; some know well the world of machines and rapid
transportation, but have had meager experience in learning the
importance of communion with others through free exchange of
thoughts and feelings. With such variances in children's backgrounds, it makes little sense to proceed with arbitrary studies
which do not recognize what children know and do not know. It
makes a great deal of sense to plan studies which use the content
of children's backgrounds to move toward deeper understandings
and new areas of experience.

First the teacher must discover what children already know. He
does so in these and similar ways:

observing children as they work and play indoors and outdoors;
listening to children share personal experiences;
analyzing children's writing and drawings and paintings;
raising points for discussion, and probing with questions to uncover
   the extent of their experiences;
conducting informal oral and written tests.

When the teacher discovers gaps in group understanding, he may
plan a study to help correct the situation:

The children had weekly allowances, and many material advantages including house-pets and private swimming pools. They constantly reported lack of money to buy things which struck their fancy. It seemed to me they did not much value using money carefully. I felt that a study related to money and banking might be helpful, if the group could be interested. I wanted to emphasize these understandings:

We must decide what we wish to purchase with money.
We need to make long-term plans for the use of money.
Banks help some people to save money, while they help others to use money for important purchases.

In another situation the teacher was surprised to hear during a sharing period how fearfully the group responded to the news of a classmate's going to the hospital. It seemed clear that the group did not understand that illness was a normal part of life and that society has ways of helping ill people—hospitalization, advances in medicine, medical specialists—all part of the goal of learning to accept oneself as a worth-while person. Discovering gaps in children's understanding provides the teacher with reasons for choosing content which will allow direct attack upon improving the situation. The question here for teachers to raise is: What kinds of studies and experiences might be valuable for this group to fill in gaps in their social understanding and development? Understanding children's backgrounds gives the teacher another sound basis for choosing appropriate content.

CRITERION FIVE: RELATIONSHIP TO TEACHER INTERESTS AND CONCERNS

What a teacher selects from the possibilities open to him depends in large measure upon his own interests and concerns. Even the gaps in children's understanding which a teacher recognizes and considers important will be related to his own personal awareness of the social world in general and the class group in particular. This does not mean that the teacher necessarily follows whims or thoughtless impulses, but only that teachers' interests, like those of children, must be recognized in determining content for study. Hence the teacher's interests and concerns make a fifth criterion to use in content selection.

Teachers have their own backgrounds of experience; they are

constantly meeting new challenges related to their teaching. Recent reading of a book like *What We Need To Know About Communism,* by the Overstreets, or Ashley Montagu's essays on cooperation may inspire a teacher to work with his group to help them recognize some fundamental differences between communism and democracy. Recent study of the increase in travel among Americans might inspire a teacher to help his group study the importance of sound "travelership." A trip abroad may result in enthusiasm for sharing some of the cultural discoveries made. In the words of one teacher: "I had spent that summer in Italy visiting my grand-uncle. I was not only excited by my visit but full of feeling for the Italian people."

When the teacher himself has keen interest in a study, he gives it personal meaning which in turn stimulates children to reach for a study which will have personal meaning for them, too. To disregard the personal resources of the teacher by preselecting study content for him denies the study topics and reality of contagious enthusiasm.

A study stressing the need for our government to help improve world conditions through shared leadership can be achieved through focus upon the Japanese as effectively as through focus upon the Argentinians or another people. The choice should be the teacher's and should depend upon his particular background of traveling and study experiences, and upon his particular interests and concerns. Only then can selections be both timely and significant for all involved. The question here is, Which of the teacher's interests and concerns might lead to the most meaningful and rewarding studies for the group involved? The teacher who regards his own interests and concerns as a valid reason for considering content, possesses inner sources of energy to use in doing his best teaching.

CRITERION SIX: AVAILABILITY OF REALISTIC
   MATERIALS FOR STUDY

Content absorbed from contacts with the living environment, from deep sensory impressions and reflections gained from the use of realistic materials, has no substitute. Direct contacts with the basic resources for learning—people in the flesh, objects in the concrete, actual processes in operation, original documents in print —make a difference not only in how children learn but in the content selected for learning. Hence the use of realistic materials offers a sixth criterion for selection of content.

People have many personal experiences and much personalized information which stimulate choice of study. They may be artists, actors, writers, diplomats, teachers, missionaries, scientists, steel workers, or horticulturists. They may be children with specialized experiences.

Denise was listed on the class roll as a non-citizen. The teacher noticed this and in questioning her found that the family would receive final papers in a month. What better time, thought the teacher, to delve into a study of naturalized citizenship, with the values and conflicts related to such a status.

Activities in the community often influence a study choice as, for example, when construction begins on a highway, new collections are added to the museum, city maps are revised, or an industry is changed. These are realistic materials, which mass-produced textbooks can never be. As compilations or recapitulations of others' impressions, textbooks are far removed from the original sources of information. They are far too condensed to allow detailed reliving of others' experience in a degree sufficient for realistic understanding. In this sense they should not be used to influence the choice of study, even though they may contain some material useful in pursuing certain studies.

By relying instead upon "living" materials, teachers have a rich source from which to choose study content. The question here is, What in the surrounding environment, within the classroom and outside, can be used to help select meaningful, significant content for study? By keeping alert to school and community resources, the teacher gains new possibilities for making appropriate choices.

CRITERION SEVEN: SATISFACTION OF LEGAL REQUIREMENTS AND EXPERT OPINION

No teacher stands alone in his opinions and judgment. Years of college study, continuous professional reading, participation in workshops, seminars, and conferences all contribute toward adequate selection of content. Teachers, like others, are influenced by expert opinion. Specialists in social sciences, consultants, and other teachers all profit by discussing apppropriate content for study. Teachers become stimulated as they study guides, bulletins, and other professional reading materials.

Nevertheless, the final choice rightfully belongs to the teacher. With a common core of objectives clearly in mind, he is in a strategic position to decide with his group what the most productive content for study will be. This is both the teacher's right and his responsibility. Teachers may not be free to choose whether or not to teach toward socially acceptable goals, but as professional workers they must be permitted to choose the particular understandings and content for study. To do otherwise imperils their professional status. Whenever teachers are expected to follow uniform studies, they have little incentive for thinking through content significant for their groups. The fact that teacher representatives contributed to the selection of content which became required of all does not render such content less rigid and frozen, less untimely and inappropriate for a particular group.

In spite of restrictions, many teachers recognize the need to branch out and sharpen their focus for study and find means of doing so. Miss Ford was one of these.

I felt strongly that the required study of pioneers—the cowboy and Indian theme—had been sufficiently part of the group's experience not to repeat it. I also felt that pioneering was a way of life more than a migration westward. I asked the children to draw their ideas of pioneers; most showed them in buckskins, toting guns and riding in covered wagons. I deliberately led the group toward a discussion and plans for a study of pioneering as a modern concept of exploration—in medicine, in the African move toward independence, in Antarctica, in America of today and yesterday.

Mrs. Medford was another who used a "requirement" as a point from which to move outward.

We were discussing the Revolutionary War as outlined in the text. "Why did the colonists fight the war?" was the question on the page where the answer was, "They wanted their freedom." I asked what freedom meant and became fascinated by the response. The children chose to talk about the Negro situation and its relationship to freedom. The possibility for an intensive study of freedom formed in my mind—working on the idea of understanding the place of the individual in a democracy—that democracy grows as more people gain personal and governmental rights; that individuals need to use their intelligence and resources to solve group problems.

There are those who believe that teachers are inadequately educated and too inexperienced to select content; yet these same people are willing to allow them to work intimately and privately with students, expressing their own personalities and ways of teaching. Are decisions of content more important than those of interpersonal relationships and processes of learning? May not responsibility for selection of content increase the sense of responsibility for meaningful teaching and constructive relating to children? Some people fear that, free to select content, teachers will choose blindly or unintelligently; they fear that children will suffer from repeated content or insignificant learnings. These dangers are real, but exist regardless of who selects content. Who better than teachers can work closely with children to plan content which is neither repetitious nor insignificant? The dangers of imbalance are simply increased when teachers do not take responsibility for judging the appropriateness of content for study.

The question here is, How can the legalities of the situation and local requirements be adapted to allow for the selection of content which best meets all the criteria for selection? When administrators expect teachers to choose wisely and stand ready to assist them, and when teachers are expected to justify for themselves their choices of content, they have reason for working creatively. They have a reason for learning to recognize that society, children, teachers, materials, legalities, all carry weight in determining the selections of content for study.

Chapter III

MAKING CHOICES OF PROCEDURES

WHAT CHILDREN EXPERIENCE DURING THEIR SEARCH FOR INFORMA-
tion makes for content-learning, which may be as significant as the
content-learning of findings themselves. As children react to facts
and materials and people, they gain the content of understandings,
impressions, and feelings which become values for action. They
learn to feel the things they know and know the things they feel;
in this way knowing and feeling cannot be separated. Consequently
the procedures for study must be selected carefully. When procedures are planned in terms of the understandings and expected
outcomes to be achieved, children will have continuous opportunity to think, feel, value, and behave as intelligent human beings.

Generating a Study

Planning in this sense begins with the manner in which a study
is generated and the purposes for study are identified.

IDENTIFYING IDEAS FOR STUDY

When the teacher allows emerging conditions rather than pre-
planned unit-content to become the basic sources of study, any
number of situations may serve as sparks for identifying content
for study.

Pressing problems or challenges. Frequently during the school
year natural problems arise which can be capitalized upon for
study. The class is informed that it will have responsibility for an
assembly program during Public Schools Week months hence. The
Board of Education asks the class to think through suggestions for

planning a new school. The group's week for outdoor camping is soon to arrive. Donations of clothing for foreign children are requested by a welfare organization.

Situations like these can lead to all sorts of studies yielding significant understandings—understanding the relationships between public schools and the goals of our democracy or understanding how society plans so that people's free time may be used constructively; or recognizing the role of voluntary organizations. Pressing problems sometimes appear as once-in-a-lifetime opportunities; sometimes they occur regularly and can be anticipated. In either case they offer realistic study in which intelligent action can be taken.

Developing points of discussion. There are many discussions which sometimes, arising spontaneously and in unplanned fashion, provoke genuine curiosity. Questions and disagreements often give clues for significant study. A group discussing a certain television program begins to argue the relative merits of programs. Issues such as the values and limitations of television arise, or reasons for the kinds of programs existing and needs for improved standards are pursued. In either case an emerging study might emphasize the larger idea of recognizing how the individual can make wise choices for his use of time.

Free discussions will occur only when the teacher allows them and values them for stimulating thinking. Curiosity in the classroom can either be stifled or be given the necessary impetus to move the group to deeper study.

Leads from ongoing studies. There are times during a study when leads to new studies emerge as a natural consequence. A group studying prejudice looks at individual and family prejudices among others. Awareness of differences among the group comes to the surface in sufficient degree for the teacher to consider the possibility of moving the group toward a study concerning self-assessment—understanding and accepting oneself as a worth-while person. Study of the library as a place of learning leads to study of another learning agency, the museum—both part of the idea of understanding the ways individuals get their education. A study of hospitalization suggests interest in the work of doctors and their specialties in a world of technological advancements. Many times ongoing studies, if not too broad or exhaustive, offer attractive leads to emphasize another understanding.

Planned presentations. There may be definite times when the teacher preplans an experience, hoping to arouse discussion and thought. The teacher announces to the group that he would like to share some slides and purchases made in Mexico during his summer trip. His goal is to discover some clues to children's interest in understanding the people there and their problems. Or the teacher may read the story *Make Way for the Ducklings* to the group, intending to stimulate thought about city traffic conditions and how people make provisions for safety. If sufficient concern is aroused, such a study might concentrate upon the goal of realizing the importance of using human resources wisely. When the teacher has a particular reason for trying out a study idea for group reaction, he should feel free to do so. The results may or may not suggest leads to study.

Test situations. Teachers gather clues to study needs by inventories, interviews, staged role-playing situations, and informal examinations. In these ways teachers probe children's concepts and attitudes. For example, a teacher asks children to tell what they know about the "community" as she records the responses. She then asks them to respond to pictures on community life. She invites them to list places they have lived and visited. From the information gathered she may discover that the children perceive the concept in terms of the impersonal aspect of supplying materialistic basic needs such as food, clothing, and shelter, but not in terms of people' contributions to effective group living. Although she may feel obligated to work in the area of community life, she wishes to emphasize new learnings, perhaps working toward the goal of understanding the role of volunteer organizations and services in democratic living—that people develop groups of many kinds to satisfy their needs and promote their interests.

Another teacher arranges a role-playing situation for children to demonstrate what they think are the most important rules for people to live by. He wants to discover some needs for study in the area of laws and rules, an area of strong personal appeal to him. He hopes such a study will involve the big idea of recognizing the need for group control of individual action—that in all groups there are patterns of approved conduct, some formally defined, some informal but generally accepted.

When used in this manner, rather than to determine gains at the end of a study, test situations become profitable beginning steps to spark a study.

Direct appeals for suggestions. Many times a direct question in which the teacher honestly seeks opinions and suggestions for study brings astonishing results. The teacher says to the group, "If you could choose what to study in regard to people, what would your choice be and why? Think about it today; talk it over. Tomorrow we will hear your choices." The next day brings various proposals, among them one which seems to arouse a strong interest —studying the people of the two new states: what they are like, why their territories joined the United States, and what problems they face. The teacher recognizes an opportunity to emphasize understanding of the role of group action in a democracy—that in a democracy people use their government to meet new needs created by change and growth.

Without prompting, children often request studies, if the teacher is willing to listen. One group informally asks their teacher if they may study the Eastern States Exposition being planned in their community. When the teacher in turn asks what value such a study might have, the children cite better understanding of the reasons for expositions and how they are run. The teacher thinks of the goal—understanding the role of voluntary organizations and government in the world of work—that people of like occupations and economic interests often unite to work toward common goals. Not every spark proposed by children can be nurtured into a significant study, of course; nor should it be. Whether the spark originates with one member of the group, with the teacher, or with the entire group, final choices are made by everyone, thinking together and free to exercise judgment in decision-making.

Outside requirements. There are times when the choice of a study must fit an outside requirement. Children have the right to be told this and not be fooled into thinking they have a choice to make. The danger lies, not in occasional fulfillment of outside requirements—children can accept this reality, especially when they feel a strong identification with the teacher—but in the compliant attitude and nonthinking habit formed by constant dependence upon authoritarian sources. Accustomed to having someone else do their "big" thinking and planning, children often learn to *enjoy* being told what to do, and feel lost when they are confronted with decision-making responsibility.

No matter who generates the spark for a particular study, however, the important thing is whether the spark is fanned into flames of honest enthusiasm which becomes identified with significant goals for study.

IDENTIFYING PURPOSES FOR STUDY

Making choices of content for study does not mean irresponsible, out-of-the-hat procedure. Both teachers and pupils must feel that the study carries purposes significant to them. Both must know why they are pursuing a particular study.

Purposes which teachers recognize need not be apparent to pupils. Teachers have long-range goals of understanding and behavior which immature learners cannot fully share. They express those goals in adult terms. Children are concerned more with immediate goals of study and action, expressed in terms which they best understand. Building an airport for dramatic play, making preparations for camping, organizing a program for parents—such goals often become sufficient reason for children to search out information and practice skills. Not to be overlooked is the simple goal of being allowed to explore their questions arising out of curiosity, so that they may satisfy hunger for learning.

While teachers' and pupils' goals need not be identical, they should be compatible. Each group should accept the other's purposes for what they are. This is best done through cooperative planning.

Planning Cooperatively

By setting goals together, teachers and pupils can evaluate progress continuously as a group endeavor.

THE TEACHER'S RESPONSIBILITY

The teacher preplans by becoming clearly aware of the outcomes to be achieved and the criteria to be used in selecting content. He keeps abreast of current affairs, accumulating background data on various social issues and problems and maintaining files of materials. He explores the range of studies which might have personal meaning for children. But he goes no further without consultation with the group. He does not prepare a teaching unit in which personal stake in preparation takes precedence over the group's interest and ability to identify with the topic. He does not deny children's right to practice choice-making.

This does not mean the teacher sits idly by, letting children grope and struggle endlessly with vague ideas. Children cannot always articulate their interests and ideas without help and practice. They do not always recognize alternatives without guidance. Obviously the teacher is there to assist, to take active responsibility for drawing out the group's thinking and, if necessary, alerting its members to possibilities for study and action.

By proceeding slowly and probing carefully, teachers gain time to learn children's reactions and to gauge their ability to handle and grasp the ideas involved. They feel free to "forget" proposals that were not accepted enthusiastically. In this kind of atmosphere children do not hesitate to show their interest or lack of it; they feel free to reveal their true abilities and inabilities. At no time, however, need the teacher fear losing control of the situation. Intentionally or not, he maintains control by the kinds of questions asked, suggestions picked up, and the opportunities given for thinking through the factors in choice-making and agreement-reaching. He does not in any sense abdicate control in cooperative planning, but maintains it by showing faith in children's ability to share responsibility for thinking and action.

There are several misconceptions regarding cooperative planning which should be cleared up. For one, cooperative planning does not mean that the teacher always asks, never tells. There are times when it is both necessary and desirable for teachers to give their reasons and ideas, their cautions and disapprovals. What counts is the honest give-and-take between group members and teacher, and the total number of opportunities given to children to make intelligent decisions concerning study content and process.

Cooperative planning does not necessarily limit itself to voting. Without sufficient discussion of a question, voting carries little meaning. More basic to cooperative planning than voting is interaction of group members to evaluate alternatives and reach agreement whenever possible.

Nor does cooperative planning mean that the entire group must be involved every step of the way. Intelligent planning is not always best accomplished in large-group situations. There are times when a small group or certain individuals must take heavier responsibility than others for group planning. Children, like adults, vary in the kinds of thinking they do best. Faced with a variety of planning situations, each child will seek his level of intelligent participation. What becomes important is for all children to have opportunity to learn and use group planning skills and to value the opportunities to do so.

Opportunities for Cooperative Planning

Cooperative planning occurs throughout a study at times like these:

When selecting content:

thinking through the significance of proposals;
considering alternatives and consequences for action;
raising questions and suggestions.

When deciding upon purpose and goals for study:

clarifying what is to be achieved;
clarifying immediate goals as steps along the way;
accepting commitments for contributions and efforts;
determining the questions or problem to be pursued.

When deciding upon materials for study:

listing and collecting sources of information;
carrying through commitments;
evaluating usefulness of materials for purposes set up.

When deciding upon procedures:

choosing effective techniques for achieving purposes;
contributing to individual and team searching.

When evaluating progress:

planning ways to correct mistakes and points of confusion;
discussing individual and team contributions;
analyzing barriers to progress, such as chairman's difficulty in delegating
  responsibility, individual's difficulty in identifying with group goals,
  inaccuracy in reporting, competition for materials;
analyzing time schedules and routines set up to achieve goals.

When evaluating results:

analyzing ideas gained, achievements made;
verifying knowledge acquired by behavior shown.

Throughout a study children should be involved in thinking through questions of this nature: What do we need to know and do in order to reach our goal? What can we do to improve the present situation? What went wrong and why? These become real problems to be solved. Solving them takes time, but it is time well spent.

Mistakes occur, of course. Children can learn to profit by their mistakes and to use their intelligence to avoid further mistakes. They can learn to value the burdens of free choice as well as the privileges. While the teacher wishes to help children look ahead to consequences and to contribute his suggestions as group leader, he does not expect perfection in children's performances. He does not censure them for the mistakes they make when thinking independently.

VALUES OF COOPERATIVE PLANNING

Life demands continuous planning—how to use the day, how to reach the museum, whom to marry, what career to pursue. Children need practice to become accustomed to planning and organizing their own time and space. Although the level and kind of participation vary with experience, six-year-olds are as capable of doing effective planning as twelve-year-olds.

Young children and older ones alike experience satisfaction in carrying out plans which they have helped to make. Children of all ages have added incentive for following through the purposes which they help to establish. When they contribute their thinking in honest, free discussion, children learn to feel that what they have to say is important for others to hear. They learn to express themselves, defend their thoughts, and help a group to broaden and deepen its thinking. Cooperative planning, in short, has value for all children.

Conducting the Study

Plans sometimes change as studies develop and decisions are evaluated. But the search for information, the sources used, the meanings clarified, and the actions organized are all part of a group's cooperatively made decisions for study. While these phases of the cycle overlap and have no particular sequential order, each has its own significance.

Arranging the Search for Information

Whatever the goal of study may be, pertinent information becomes a necessary part of intelligent thinking and action. But the process of learning how to secure information is equally important. The teacher's search, however useful in securing background data, never counts as the child's search. Teaching reveals the results of the teacher's search. It may supply valuable information but fail to provide experience in learning the process of uncovering pertinent information. Assigning pages to be read and questions to answer for recitation or testing purposes may also result in information gained but, again, not in a genuine search for knowledge.

To be genuine the search requires personalized action. The searchers themselves think through the best possible sources of information for the purposes agreed upon. Different children, as well as different teachers, find different styles of working best suited to them, but all styles must be justified in terms of the purposes to be achieved.

When searches emerge. Sometimes the search unfolds in wavelike movements which build up to unified study as new reasons for continued search emerge. An example is a study of leadership through which the teacher hoped to contribute to an understanding of the role of the individual in a democracy. One of the related understandings he desired to foster was that democracy grows as more people gain the right to participate in government at all levels. A brief report of the study follows:

The first phase had for its purpose preparation for the class officers' election. A study of campaigning was involved.

The second phase of searching occurred after the election when the group looked at results. The teacher guided discussion toward a general one of leadership and summarized the group's thinking around three major questions: What problems do leaders face? How do leaders help solve people's problems? What kinds of leaders are there? Plans were made to organize discussion of questions. The group decided to work on the kinds of leaders with committees choosing various categories of leaders—in politics, the military, education, art, science, religion. Each committee had responsibility to gather materials, prepare more detailed questions for searching, and share their findings with the group.

The third phase occurred during the sharing of information. The point of local leadership in the community arose, at which time the teacher suggested this become a study for the group to undertake, perhaps by inviting local leaders to school for interviews.

While the teacher set the conditions for the first search, individual children proposed conditions for the second search—committees going further with new proposals—while for the third, the teacher again helped the group move ahead to re-searching.

Conditions for each phase of the search are sometimes pinpointed by the teacher, who judges the group interest as the study emerges. An example is a study of farm work through which the teacher hoped to contribute to a realization of how scientific advancements change ways people work. A related understanding he wished to promote was that changes due to technological progress affect the jobs people hold. Following is an account of the study:

Discussion followed the teacher's reading of a farm-life story to the group. The discussion was sufficiently animated for the teacher to put a question on the board: Who are the workers on the farm? She suggested that the group organize its thinking, and offered to prepare a chart outline for the bulletin board, using the following headings:

Farm Workers	**Work Done**	**When**

Everyone hunted for information, placing markers on pages of pertinent text or illustration. The teacher collected books for the group.

During the search she sometimes worked with a small group, while others worked on their own. As the group reported daily results, the wall chart became filled.

One day the teacher mentioned that different kinds of farms had complicated the chart-making. Should some searching be done about the kinds of farms and the work demanded? Some children volunteered to make such a list and report to the larger group. They did so in the form of a pictorial chart. Spurred by the results, other children agreed to portray one kind of farm. Their pictures were used to search out more information related to specialized farms and work demands.

Discussions turned attention to early-type farms, as some of the children shared information about their grandparents' farms. Searching took on a historical note as children sought to compare farm workers of today with those of yesterday.

Since only one question was dealt with at a time, the searching became highly concentrated. However this question was sufficiently open for all kinds of answers to be sought according to individual interest. Both *ad hoc* committee work and existing reading groups were used to expedite the group's searching.

When searches are fully mapped out. There are times when studies are fully planned before searching begins, and the searching is accomplished mainly in one concentration. An example is a study of people's prejudices. One of the teacher's goals was to help children value likenesses and differences among people and to promote the general understanding that people within a culture differ because of backgrounds of experience, family, economic levels, personal values, and capacities. A brief resumé of the study follows:

Once the group had decided upon a study of people's prejudices—the interest which the teacher had in this area was contagious—the teacher called for a group-made outline of plans for study, with this result:

I. Define prejudice.
   Read *All About Us*[1] to class.
   Write essay on meaning of prejudice.
   Make lists of family prejudices.
II. Discuss ways prejudices are formed.
   Make an opinion poll.
   Find out what films to use.
   Collect materials.

[1]Eva K. Evans, *All About Us* (New York: Golden Press, 1947).

III. Explore kinds of prejudices in committees.
    Racial.
    Political.
    Religious.
    Social.
IV. Study areas where less prejudice exists and try to discover the reasons.
V. Prepare arguments for conclusions.

Copies of outlines were prepared for everyone as the group organized for the searching. During the discussions and reporting, when new questions arose, the teacher called for volunteers to search out the question as homework and report briefly to the group, but none became major topics for study.

Instead of using outlines as the means of organizing searches for information, questions sometimes are recorded and categorized. Or individuals write questions on separate cards which are sorted. Hunches, too, become the objects of search for verification. Individuals or committees usually choose questions or categories of them to pursue further. There are times, however, when the entire group together searches out a question or questions.

A study of money was undertaken by a different class. The teacher wanted the children to take into account the factors involved in choosing and using goods and services. He wanted to develop the general understanding that we make choices in terms of past experiences, satisfactions we seek, and the resources we have. The study progressed as follows:

Noticing how carelessly the children were spending their allowances, the teacher raised the question of handling money. From the discussion he solicited questions for further study and charted them, along with suggestions for finding answers.

Study Topic: Money

Our Questions	Ways to Find Answers
What is money?	Make charts to discuss and share.
Why do we have money?	Interview parents.
Who makes money?	Draw pictures of things we are
How do families decide on ways they will spend money?	saving for.
	Visit the bank.

Our Questions	*Ways to Find Answers*
How does paying taxes help or hinder?	Make lists of ways people earn money.
Why do people save? How do they?	See a movie on saving.
Why do people work?	Build a model savings bank to act out how to save.

Here the study moved along as individuals reported the daily results of their searching on each question. When the time came to carry through their plans to construct a bank in the classroom, committees were organized to tackle the job. Sometimes an entire research revolved around only one question or concern, for example, "What are the problems in our growing community?"

When searches are broad. At times the group has no questions or problems to search out, merely a topic to explore, such as "Religions of the World," "Our City's Recreational Facilities," or "The Growing Motel Business." While the teacher has particular understandings in mind, the children search out whatever information they think is pertinent. The teacher assists by preparing guide sheets for study, or works closely with an individual or a small group needing special help. During such broad explorations the teacher is careful to help the group tie results together in a manner which leads to common understandings.

When searches are individualized. Not every study conducted need be oriented to the total group. Occasionally an individual or a small group of friends feels a concern which is unrelated to the class endeavor.

A small group of boys became fascinated with a library book they had read on city sewage systems and their importance. With the teacher's permission, they hunted down information and carried on discussions, helping one another in their search.

In such instances the teacher guides the small group's search more or less as he would a class-accepted pursuit. Other children work independently on interests and skill practice needed, as they would if the teacher were working with any committee or ability group. Sometimes small-group studies form gradually as interests grow. Here is an example:

It started out with the problem of governing themselves in the class-room. A committee agreed to study the problem and make proposals to the class. In the meantime, class discussion led to an interest in the problems of communicating with people. A group volunteered to search this further. A week or so later another general discussion stimulated the formation of a searching team on the problems of education. Still later another group emerged with responsibility for searching in the area of human relations. The teacher sensed the understandings which underlay the various groups' efforts—that men working together can solve their problems; that problems grow and change but never cease.

This kind of searching takes on an informal aspect, with individualized explorations brought together occasionally by total group sharing and discussion.

When searches are project-oriented. Searches may be undertaken for the purpose of fulfilling a planned project. A group preparing a class breakfast needs to search out information related to people's choices of food and the factors involved. Another group, preparing a telephone directory of classmates' numbers, becomes involved in the study of the purposes and uses of directories, as well as the values of telephoning as a means of communicating. Such a study focuses upon recognizing the importance of effective communicating in living today—that communication depends upon two-way understanding.

The teacher's control. While the teacher does not do the children's searching, he unavoidably controls the searching by the kinds of arrangements he permits and the kinds of questions he helps the group to select. Some arrangements allow for more practice in searching than others. When children handle many resources, they learn that single searches do not always suffice as reliable and valid means of securing information. They learn to realize that not all answers are found in books; that books themselves are only the results of other people's searching. Some questions allow for more individualized and productive thinking than others. The question, Is poverty the root of all problems in South America? stimulates more interpretative searching, especially if examples and reasons accompany conclusions, than such a question as, What do the people of South America import and export? What does war do to the people who must fight it? provokes more reflective search than, What led up to the war? Asking the right questions, and selecting those which seem most closely related to the understandings to be achieved, means the difference between hit-and-miss studies and studies which build one interest upon another in quality searching.

USING SOURCES OF INFORMATION

Once the goal of study has been defined and searches for information have been arranged, teachers and pupils share the task of gathering resources for study. An entire group's effort should naturally result in a wider range of available resources than could be gathered by the teacher alone. By participating in planning the resources to be used, children learn to explore and evaluate more skillfully for themselves what makes "best" sources of information.

Teachers help children think through adequate sources of information by keeping before them the question, How can we best get the information we need? "Best" of course depends upon many things; not only the sources but also children's experiences and styles of learning. Younger children usually have had fewer experiences for building up funds of understandings, but age does not always make the difference. Some younger children are better able to handle certain concepts than older ones whose intellect or experience might be more limited.

In reaching out toward unfamiliar areas of experience all children profit by touching and seeing for themselves and by remaining in close contact with people as basic sources of information. When working with familiar concepts all children can be helped to reflect upon their experiences, extracting deeper meanings from them through discussion and reading.

Regardless of age, children need to learn to use resources for their own independent thinking and to avoid relying upon indirect, unquestioned authority for their thinking. Thinking crutches in the form of secondhand information too often weaken a child's ability to respond to "raw" materials with confidence in himself as a thinker and as a person able to feel in direct communication with materials without outside help or interpretation. In any case, the information gained will be only as accurate and as provocative as the sources used.

Using field trips.   Field trips often serve as valuable sources of information and incentives to action.   When trips are used to help a group search out information and clarify thinking, they gain their greatest vitality as sources of learning.   To do this, of course, trips must be timed and related to the search at hand.   In the words of one teacher:

While our trip to the senate to hear debate of local problems did not provide us with all the answers, it did help us gain a perspective and deeper understanding of democratic governmental processes.   It launched us into a more meaningful study of government and gave us direction in our search for understanding the functions of the different levels of government and the relationship of these levels to one another and to us.

Oftentimes questions listed before the trip guide the searching.   They may be question posed by the group or by individuals, such as these:

Do you keep guns at the bank? (John)
Do all kinds of people use the bank? (Steve M.)
How would I get my money out of the bank? (Michael)
How much money do people put in the bank? (Janice)

Frequently questions answered by the trip stimulate further questions for searching.   A group visiting a nearby motel went with these questions:

Is the motel company-owned or owned by one person?
What does AAA mean?
How do motels protect their guests?
How are motels advertised?

The trip raised some broader questions:

Why are motels replacing hotels?
How does a motel help the community?
Why are motels built so close to each other?
What other businesses grow up in connection with motels?

Depending upon the information to be searched out, there are literally hundreds of places to be visited as sources of learning.   Among them are laundries, hotels, newspaper offices, warehouses, department stores, construction scenes—wherever children are allowed to penetrate behind the view ordinarily seen by the public. School resource files and the local chamber of commerce list innumerable possibilities.

There is no need to wear out a few places with "trips for the grade" which all children of a certain grade automatically take each year. Nor need field trips be lengthy, once-a-year affairs. A walk to the city park to survey facilities or to the corner to analyze traffic provides as much data for searching as a train ride or bus trip to a neighboring town. Whether long or short, trips not only provide possible answers to questions but stimulate social learnings which other sources may not provide. Plans need to be made by teachers and pupils, duties and routines cared for, conduct in public clarified. As they become involved in the trip's planning, children gain practice in following through their responsibilities.

The teacher too has responsibility for helping to arrange for the best possible learning conditions during the trip and after. Contacting the host to explain what the children want to learn, stating the purpose of the trip, previewing the trip if possible, acting as liaison person to clarify questions and summarize observations are some ways for the teacher to ensure a profitable trip experience. To take children on trips simply as a desirable or required activity for a study, whether or not they can search out new learnings, is meaningless. To justify the time and effort involved in using field trips, the teacher should have these questions in mind:

Will the field trip provide deeper understandings related to the problems or questions raised before the group?

Have the majority already made sufficient observations on their own or with their families so that the information can be drawn equally well from their previous experiences?

When the purpose for a trip is mutually understood and clearly to gain needed information, the field trip becomes a genuine learning resource.

Examining authentic objects and original papers. Trips provide access to things seen in relation to their functions, but there are times too when examination of objects not in use leads to answers. In this sense museums, with their rich supplies of original materials, historical documents, maps, artifacts, specimens, models, and drawings, become basic sources of information to be searched out. Other resources are to be found in samples of industrial and commercial supplies, as well as among family and other private collections.

In one classroom, children studying the old and the new, gathered copies of old McGuffey readers, old irons, and washboards. Their trip to the nearby antique shop resulted in close observation of spinning wheels, old furniture, kerosene lamps, and the like. In another classroom, children studying their cafeteria situation collected for analysis the daily menus for a week.

Whenever children examine for themselves the artifacts and original papers which encourage independent reflection, the application of the historical method of searching becomes possible. While Einstein was still alive, children studying the work of scientists wrote to him and received his written reply to use as information. A group studying school expansion secured from the architect original blueprints of the new school wing and, from the principal, reports to the board of education of the school's growth. From their parents and grandparents they collected old report cards and snapshots of schools.

Children studying problems of human relations examined a copy of the United Nations' Declaration of Human Rights. Able readers on the committee read to the less able; discerning interpreters translated the material for others. Able readers and sharp interpreters were not always the same individuals. In ways like these, children themselves investigate and handle original source materials, and begin to understand the true sources of information.

Interviewing people. Talking with people—questioning them —is perhaps one of the simpler means of securing useful and pertinent data. As a basic technique of reasearch, it can be handled by young as well as older children. In the role of researchers, children learn to prepare and conduct interviews, develop questionnaires, and draft letters of inquiry. They learn how to select the "best" people for particular kinds of information needed. They learn to evaluate people's information in terms of probable reliability and validity.

Sometimes this kind of searching is organized informally as children talk with people. They talk with their parents to learn, for example, how adults decide when to repair or buy shoes, the kind of schooling parents had, or the work they do. Children listen to one another as each explains his religion or personal differences. They invite a guest speaker to talk to them on a particular subject. They ask the teacher to share his thinking on a topic or to respond to certain questions the pupils have.

When searching is more formally organized, children prepare working sheets to guide the searching. The entire class may work together to prepare such a sheet as the following:

> I think prejudice is . . .
> I am prejudiced about . . .
> My mother is prejudiced about . . .
> My father is prejudiced about . . .

Committees sometimes take the responsibility of preparing needed research instruments.

Do you think a negative attitude toward dating between white people and Negroes is a matter of prejudice? Why?
What can we do to reduce prejudice in our classoom and elsewhere?
Please write down your answers for us to use. Thank you.

COMMITTEE ON RACIAL PREJUDICE

Individuals working on their own sometimes devise data sheets to gather specific information.

Dear Teacher:
I am making a survey to determine just what are the problems on the school playground. Will you please consult your pupils about the playground situation so that this record will be accurate?
Thank you for your help.

Pat Ryan

Grade: _____   Teacher: _____

Children's problems:

Using the equipment:

With playmates:

Other kinds:

Teacher's problems:

With children in other grades:

With children in your room:

Other kinds:

Almost any study lends itself to interviewing as a means of information-getting—asking teachers in the school and children from other rooms how they view playground problems, preparing questions to ask an engineer-father who plans to visit the class, or probing themselves to discover what certain words mean to them. Children develop the research skill of asking the "right" questions by learning to handle interviewing as a basic source of information.

Studying filmstrips, films, recordings, TV, radio. Audio-visual materials are valuable for close-range study. Films and filmstrips can be examined and re-examined, tapes and recordings heard and reheard. For certain studies, films promise the most valid and realistic information possible for young children. In the study of likenesses and differences of peoples, for example, the teacher found reading material too difficult, but located a number of up-to-date films on the children's level of understanding. The entire search was based largely upon the use of films. When the teacher orders materials, children should be informed of the purpose. When this is done well ahead of scheduled viewing time, children not only can be alerted to the search, but can help to plan the details for searching.

In a study of farm workers, the teacher prepared a bulletin board caption to use in guiding the planned film-viewing.

Worker	Kind of Work Done

As information was obtained, children dictated answers to the teacher for recording.

Children themselves often handle the search for appropriate audio-visual materials.

Each committee searched through the catalog for selections they wished to preview. They recorded their decisions on a reference chart:

General *(ordered by the teacher):* "Boundary Lines"
Racial Committee: "Americans All"
Political Committee: "House I Live In"
Social Committee: "Schools and Children Around the World"
                  "Family Life Around the World"
                  "Immigration"

Some schools have a darkroom for previewing. If there is not one, committees may preview films during lunch hour or after school, when classrooms are empty. One committee managed to set up a dark corner in a classroom. They hung up sheets to keep out the light and turned the sound low to avoid disturbing others.

Films and filmstrips function as basic sources of information for the questions and concerns at hand and not simply as afternoon "enrichment" activity. When they are used to search out information which is valid, realistic, and pertinent they become important tools of learning.

Analyzing graphic materials. As a form of audio-visual material, study prints and the like contain much information to be searched out by children. Some teachers and schools accumulate picture files. Public libraries frequently lend illustrative materials. Most children find magazines at home to contribute for class use. Magazines like *Life* and *Look, Holiday* and *National Geographic,* as well as many library books, are filled with photographs containing up-to-date, accurate, realistic information. Although both children and teachers will hunt for study pictures, teachers need to make certain that children gain pertinent information from them. Planning searches for particular kinds of pictures helps, as in the case of the group primed to search for pictures of workers who labored at night and on holidays. Children uncovered fifty different kinds of workers, including parents, the President of the United States, waitresses, firemen, and airline pilots.

At times small groups led by the teacher gather information together from selected prints. Such information is then charted or duplicated for later restudy. Or the teacher selects prints and prepares a question or caption which he clips to each picture to guide the search. For children who have difficulty in reading, this type of source offers material which they can handle without bogging down in their search. When occasions arise for the entire class to share prints and drawings, opaque and overhead projectors make the viewing easier.

Children's own illustrations, sketches, and drawings become valuable resources in searching out information gained from past personal experiences.

The group studying freedom and its limitations used individual responses recorded in sketch form as basis for group discussions. Among the sketches were these:

freedom of speech:	except when we say something that hurts someone else
	except when we endanger our country
freedom to vote:	except when we are underage
	except when we are not registered
freedom to work:	except, for some jobs, when we are not union members
	except when we are not trained for the job

Young children especially can be encouraged to search out their past experiences through drawings, some of them to be projected for more intensive group searching. Children analyzing hospital experiences through painting and story writing responded with:

My sister Sandra was scalded with coffee. She had to go to the hospital.

When I went to the hospital I got my tonsils out. I did not get to see my tonsils.

"Homemade" globes and maps provide basic information when developed for purposes of searching. Children studying their district's schools delegated a committee to work out a large wall map of the town's schools to be used as reference. Children studying undersea explorations prepared an "atlas" of continents and oceans to identify information found.

Commercially prepared globes and maps also have a place in searching out appropriate information, when children are free to pull down wall maps and handle globes for individual and small group work. Globes belong in all classrooms, from kindergarten up, so that children can begin early to acquire geographic concepts of the earth's shape and size.

In their study of children around the world, the group had many occasions for using globes in their searching. When the entire class was involved, the teacher borrowed three other globes to allow for groups to work simultaneously.

Whether commercially prepared or constructed by the children as original materials, graphic sources of information serve as important aids to children searching for information.

Reading print. Most schools provide a variety of readers, social studies texts, encyclopedias, and other printed matter which can be combed for information. Libraries supply many books and pamphlets containing valuable content for searching. Newspapers and magazines, both children's and adults', are further sources of printed materials.

In their search for signs of prejudice, children found newspaper headlines by the dozens:

Prejudice Branded as Mental Disorder
Marriage Bill OK'd
Law to Curb Anti-Integration Force Asked
Indians Ask Support Abroad in Fight for Florida Land

Older children may prepare bibliographies of printed sources, using larger reference charts to record the materials. At times a committee prepares a worksheet to be duplicated for everyone; at other times individuals work out separate lists. Younger children simply place markers in materials where information is found. Sometimes the teacher prepares a "bibliography sheet" for children to fill in:

Name of Book	Picture or Story	Pages

Many children write original "books," dictating them if necessary, for others to use as sources of information. "What Freedom Means to Me" and "Undersea Explorers" are representative titles. Sometimes older children are invited to write materials in book or story form for younger children in the school. Or the teacher prepares some simple reading material to be duplicated for individual, committee, or group use.

When the task of gathering printed materials becomes a shared responsibility, time must be set aside for it. Days or weeks may be devoted to the task, with odd times of the day used to advantage. Teachers need especially to be prepared for emergencies when children do not carry through their intentions. By calling upon several volunteers, instead of only one, by assisting children as they attempt to write letters and stories, and by stressing the importance of dependability, teachers help children to meet their commitments for compiling materials.

During the times of searching, the teacher too acquires background information and contributes materials for searching, being careful, however, not to dominate the situation. Some teachers feel that studies cannot be carried out without ample printed material. However helpful, print is by no means indispensable to a study. Oftentimes information which, because of its recency, has not yet found its way into text or reference books, must be searched out through other sources, not always printed ones. To rely too heavily on print may mean depriving children of learning to search for up-to-date information. It may mean, too, crowding out the experience of dealing with the many sources of basic information in terms of the questions and curiosities to be answered.

Thus reading must not be made synonymous with social studies. Teaching for depth learning will occur when all the sources of information contribute toward the search for understanding.

CLARIFYING MEANINGS

However children's search for information is organized and whatever materials are gathered, the meanings absorbed from the process count most in the quality of learning experiences. As children express themselves in speech and action, they give clues to the extent of their learnings, provided the atmosphere is encouraging. In an atmosphere where children feel free to speak and act without fear of ridicule and punishment for being wrong, they can afford to respond on their true level of thinking; they can afford to appeal for help in building significant social meanings. When they trust their teacher, they will give him valid clues for action. Knowing these clues, the teacher can plan to clear up points of confusion and redirect illogical thinking. He can work to correct misconceptions and reinforce accurate meanings.

In order to obtain such clues, of course, the teacher must also plan to follow up searching activities with opportunities for children to reveal what they know and do not know as result of the searching. Children may record, construct, act, or talk it over. Whatever the plan, time should be given to sift the information gleaned, interpret it, and organize the results.

Records. In the process of recording what they have learned from their searching, children gain time to reflect upon their learning experiences and to organize them. Records are made with pencil, crayon, paintbrush, chalk. They take shape in written response.

Following the children's survey of playground problems, the teacher said, "Write down the problems you now see in regard to the playground situation." Sometime later, after the visit by the physical education consultant, the teacher's instructions were, "From what Mr. Perkins told us, write down what you found a good physical education program should accomplish."

Records also take shape in chart form.

After a discussion involving uses of money, the teacher said, "Think of at least two things people need and two things people want, to add to our chart."

Things We Use Money For

Needs	*Wants*

Records take shape as a list.

After interviews with parents on tax monies, children were told by the teacher, "Make a list of all the ways you found tax money to be used. Do it with drawings or words or both, as you wish."

Records can be in the form of letters.

After the visit to the bank, thank-you letters were written in which the teacher asked the children to ". . . mention something important which you learned."

Pictures and stories become useful records.

Following a discussion of *The Story of Madeline,* which the teacher read to the class, the teacher suggested to the children, "Draw pictures or paint them and write a story about some part of our little French friend's experience with hospitals."

Sketches serve as brief records.

As a result of their visit to the shoe repair shop, the children were asked to sketch the different parts of the shoemaker's day as they recalled it.

Formal written reports become more permanent records, with titles like "Progress in South America."

Individual responsibility of this sort is usually handled independently while the teacher works with small groups in other content or skill areas, or in relation to other social studies tasks of the group. When some individuals complete their recording before others do, they assemble in small sharing groups with their own chairman or the teacher—or no chosen leader at all. This procedure not only saves time for fuller discussions and other important common experiences later, but stimulates intensive interaction.

Frequently a small group collectively takes responsibility for a record in the form of a report, chart, movie, play, or even duplicated guide sheets to be used in larger group discussions.

A small group volunteered to write a class constitution during a study of civil liberties; another group chose to prepare a bill of rights to be submitted to the total class for analysis and discussion.

At times quizzes and "test" situations, instruction cards for role-playing of conflicts, or open-ended stories are prepared by individuals or committees or the teacher. One teacher prepared such a role-playing device.

Mr. Young was choosing students to play certain parts in the school play. He had to choose "actors" for the following parts: (1) a brave and kind character, (2) a person saying foolish things, (3) a good dancer and singer, (4) a cook, and (5) a servant.

1. Which one of the following students do you think should play the brave and kind main character?

Jose   David   Alice   Margarita

2. Who should be the person saying foolish things?

Barbara   Joe   Carlos   Lisa

3. Who should be the good dancer and singer?

        Albert   Mariana   Diana   Juan

4. Who should be the crook?

        Gail   Manuel   Ellena   Fred

5. Who should be the servant?

        Jackson   Hilda   Miguel   Ethel

Used in this way, inventories and evaluation devices have the purpose of clarifying and extending meanings, rather than culminating a study.

As reports and test situations are shared, some teachers like to make notes similar to the following to use in later discussions.

From Children's Reports (From a study relating to the people of Alaska)	**Understandings and Meanings** (Emphasizing ideas of change)
I. Homes, food, shelter: igloos, huts, apartments houses like ours	In urban areas, living is much like ours, even if climate is colder.
treat-muktuk drying fish	Older way to preserve food (discuss)
II. Work people do Canning (history) Hunting	Newer method of preserving food (Show pictures of canneries in operation)
Fishing—"oldest industry in territory"	Changes made from fishing for food to fishing for livelihood

When individual or committee reports are carefully spaced, one or two during a session, the teacher has time to pursue meanings and extend understandings to deeper levels of significance. Group records made by the entire class during general discussions also help to focus thinking. Individuals or committees may prepare class books for group use. Copies are duplicated in order that each class member may have his own, or books are made large enough for easy handling by children. Titles may read: "Recommended TV Viewing," "Industries on the Move," or "Freedom."

Wall charts are another way for a group to record results of its searching. Children working individually or in committees usually take responsibility for production of these charts. An example might be:

Qualities of Good Leaders	Qualities of Poor Leaders	Problems Leaders Face
Can take suggestions	Cheat others	Enforcing rules
Are trustworthy and loyal	Are cruel and greedy	Making better laws
Use their wisdom	Don't judge wisely	Making better living conditions
Want to be leaders	Pay no attention to laws	

Or the teacher sets the form and children help to fill in the information.

Working Hours for People:

> Children at school.
> Children at home.
> Shopkeepers.
> Doctors and dentists.
> Mothers at home.
> Salespeople.
> Roadbuilders.

At times, the teacher handles chartmaking, taking dictation from the group.

What a Nurse Does:

> Gives medicine to sick people.
> Takes food to patients.
> Looks in girls' mouths.
> Gives shots.
> Sees if children are out of bed.
> Runs to children when they cry.

Group records made for the purpose of clarification should be kept simple, since they are not made for "show" but as an aid to organize results of searching. Having children copy group-prepared records for individual seatwork misses the purpose of chartmaking and results in little more than busywork. The value of records, whether done individually or as group endeavor, lies not in marks and grades or in that they are "something to do," but in their usefulness for launching discussions and pinning down understandings.

Construction. Results of searching may be worked out through construction activities. Bulletin boards help children to test their understandings as they work either alone or together to prepare displays.

Sometimes volunteers contribute to a display. One such display, entitled, "In the Air We Now Find . . .," called for special contributions. Under the title on the empty bulletin board the teacher wrote:

Who will make these for our display? Put your name by the one you choose.

Blimp fliers
Missiles (unmanned)
Rockets (unmanned)
Airplane pilots
Helicopter pilots
Jet pilots

Or, a committee may take charge.

A group volunteered to make a large map of the community to show various recreational facilities. Other children would then be invited to fill in the information pictorially.

Sometimes all bulletins boards are divided among committees.

Committee	Bulletin Board
Schools Long Ago	Northwest
Schools in Totalitarian Nations	Northeast
School Conditions	South
Schools of Tomorrow	East

During both the planning stage and the sharing of bulletin board productions, teachers will want to help children clarify their ideas. Displays of objects made of clay, cardboard, paper, or fabric give children further satisfaction in developing their ideas in tangible form.

Sometimes committees choose the same form of display.

Dioramas of rural and urban living conditions in Mexico were prepared in cardboard boxes. Papier mâché and clay objects made by the children were placed inside. Stories to explain them were pinned to the sides of the boxes. Each committee chose a different scene.

Varied forms of display may be used.

The committee on the Pioneer Section of the proposed class museum decided to erect a still scene with background mural. The committee on Spacemen chose to prepare cardboard models and a scrapbook, while the committee on animal exhibits (taxidermy) decided to try their hand at stuffing a toy animal and preparing an illustrated chart of the taxidermist's work. Each committee also worked through plans for guiding visitors on "museum tours."

A committee may take full responsibility for a class project.

Some children volunteered to construct the class bank with wooden crates and brown kraft paper.

A committee may work through a project unrelated to the total group's work.

The boys who were interested in building a town's sewage system worked with straws and cardboard sheets and boxes.

To make fullest use of such projects for clarifying meanings, teachers will want to encourage children to write explanations, captions, and reports to accompany the construction, or to prepare for discussions of their work.

Construction activities can frequently be related to preparation of dramatic play situations or special programs which can be opportunities to help children intellectualize their experiences.

In making plans to turn their room into a "hospital," the group dictated items to be put on tagboard charts:

Our Hospital

We need four rooms:	We need materials
operating room	lumber
waiting room	nails
ward	paint
kitchen	tools
We need an ambulance	boxes
	thread
We need uniforms for doctors and nurses	needles
	cloth

As children work out problems of construction and plans for "playing," they often clarify meanings for themselves. Their conversations as they work together often stimulate mutual assistance. Children willingly ask each other questions which may not be posed to the teacher. When construction activities are prepatterned or when teachers take too strong a hand in guiding the project, the opportune moments for building meanings often escape.

Dramatization. In the dramatic play which sometimes follows construction activities, teachers find abundant clues to the level of children's understandings. When children dramatize situations spontaneously in their own words or prepare their own scripts, they are able to show what they think and know. (Commercially prepared scripts or highly structured play do not reveal such clues.)

Dramatization may be in relation to a real situation.

The "registrar of voters" invited children to register for election day voting. "Campaign managers" conducted campaign strategy with posters and skits. "Candidates" prepared speeches. The Election Committee prepared the "polls," "ballots," and "ballot boxes." On "election day" only registered voters voted. Ballots were counted and winners announced.

Dramatization may relate to a planned program.

Our Plans

We will have an Old-Fashioned Day
We won't use: lights
                pencil sharpener
                phonograph
                electric clock
                playground equipment
We will use: wind-up clock
                cowbell
                McGuffey readers
Girls will wear sunbonnets and make rag dolls.
Boys will build benches and stools.
We will bring our lunches—sandwiches, apples, and milk.
We will bake brownies.

Dramatization may involve only a small group at a time.

We fix:	*Shine, Shine*
shoes	We shine shoes.
saddles	We charge 2¢.
bridles	We accept tips.
belts and holsters	We will give our money to CARE.
purses	
Bring your repair jobs to us. We fix all kinds of leather goods.	

Teachers and occasionally children not involved at the time observe for evidences of correct and incorrect, old and new concepts and understandings which need to be discussed.

Many situations calling for dramatization and are impromptu presentations require no props.

During a discussion of trials in relation to civil liberty, the point of justice arose. The teacher quickly called for some volunteers to act out a scene of accusation without trial and others to act out a scene with trial. Desks and chairs were moved out of the way or became "props." The two scenes were evaluated and re-enacted.

For younger children, building blocks serve as handy prop material for impromptu situations.

A discussion relating to the use of the cafeteria led the group to agree to "practice" lunchroom ordering and manners. Volunteers quickly placed some building blocks to mark off the "cafeteria." Others collected a few trays and utensils from the cafeteria. And the play began. Eventually everyone who wished had a turn as either "seller" or "buyer."

Many older children wish to write a play or skit. At times the entire group enjoys contributing to such writing; at other times a committee takes responsibility.

The committee comparing schools in a democracy and in a totalitarian nation decided to write a play of a day in a Nazi school and a day in an American school. It was acted out as the committee's report.

Dramatization becomes a naturally satisfying experience and one which gives free play to children's efforts to organize their understandings. It is best viewed as one useful technique to help children develop significant meanings.

Discussions. Learnings are brought to the awareness level when children talk over their experiences. Whether children re-create experiences through records, construction, or dramatization, some form of verbalization becomes necessary. Verbalization without sufficient basic experience, of course, turns into empty talk. But experiences unaccompanied by talk remain incomplete and unfulfilled in an intellectual sense. The stress on doing as a basis for learning was never meant to displace talking things over, but to strengthen talk with substance. Articulate individuals are in the best position to exercise their intellectual powers.

Talking it over takes place in total group discussions, small group discussions, and conversations between two persons. The teacher usually serves as catalyst, opening up channels for thinking, raising questions for analysis, and encouraging critical inquiries. Skillful questioning by the teacher does much to sharpen children's thinking. General questions like these help:

If this is done, what could happen?
What other possible answers are there?
How do you feel about this?
What does this mean to you?
What is your thinking about this? Why do you think that?
Why did you choose this?
What help does this give us?
What would you have done?
What do you need to know before answering that?

Specific questions related to the topic or study also can be probing:

Can we change to a different church? When would we want to?
How would we accept a Negro teacher or pupil in our class?
Why do some people find it so hard to be honest?
How can you tell whether prices are fair or not?
What do you mean when you say, "That's cheap."?

While children's questions usually relate to their interests and curiosities, the teacher's questions relate more closely to the understandings he hopes children will achieve. One teacher, concerned with helping children value likenesses and differences among people, listed some discussion points made following various film viewings:

Similarities	*Differences*
of farm chores in Sweden and America	in some kinds of dancing between city living and farm living in European countries
of dress except for celebrations in European countries and America	in language
of games	in historical surroundings
in children's stories	in appearance of Caucasians and Orientals
	between ways of doing things in the Orient and in America

The teacher then made some comments about the discussions:

We talked about the close ties we have with Europeans because of our ancestry; we also talked about the need to understand the Asians. We talked of learning other languages as we grow up and planning to save our money to visit other countries. I hoped children absorbed these understandings:

Wherever they live, children usually share in family responsibilities.
Wherever they live, parents usually take good care of their children.
Some families everywhere live under impoverished conditions.
Visiting one another's countries helps to bring people closer together.
Almost every nation has its modern city life which may contrast sharply with village-living.

Giving many individuals a chance to respond on their own level of feeling and thinking becomes important in discussion periods. Calling out names before posing questions restricts the spread of thinking, as does asking questions which have only one answer. Care must be taken to invite honest discussion. Children often "give teacher what she wants" in their attempt to please, if teachers insist upon fishing for answers compatible with their own thinking.[1] Without guidance and practice, children will hardly become aware of traps in generalizing and making statements unconditionally. One teacher, for example, left these children's statements unchallenged:

Policemen always help you.
You can trust policemen—even with secrets.
Policemen teach you right from wrong.

Questions which might have stimulated critical thought were never asked, questions like:

When and whom do policemen fail to help?
What if secrets are against the law?
What is right? What is wrong? Is the law always right?
Does a policeman always know what's right or wrong?
Does the policeman teach?

Teachers themselves fall easily into traps when they fail to take time to probe children's responses. Sometimes what the teacher

[1]See Jules Henry, "Docility or Giving Teacher What She Wants," *Journal of Social Issues,* 11 (No. 2, 1955), pp. 33-41.

assumes the remark to mean may not be the child's meaning at all.

There are times when the teacher guides discussion with prepared material which he feels is particularly related to the group's study. A teacher involved with his group in a study of freedom duplicated a series of famous quotations on the subject, hoping to arouse some debate.

There are times, too, when discussions are profitably turned into small buzz sessions, with the children brought together as a full group for interpretations. Occasionally children interested in exploring a question more thoroughly join with the teacher or a small group for extended discussions which may or may not be brought back to the larger group.

Small discussion groups are sometimes organized on a more formal basis, with the class divided into three or four groups functioning simultaneously. Teachers circulate to catch points in the various conversations, pose provocative questions, or simply take notes for use in larger group discussions.

Teachers sometimes worry about the noise factor during such periods of interaction. While they rightly encourage children to keep their voices down, some noise becomes inevitable, even desirable, as children explain and test their ideas with one another. Much mutual learning occurs as children exchange ideas among themselves and talk over problems.

The teacher need not always function as group leader during discussions. At times group members or committees take charge of discussions, serving as chairmen or panel experts. While the teacher may work with the individual or a committee to help them prepare for the responsibility, he acts mainly as resource person during such discussions.

Clarifying meanings becomes an easier task with small groups of course. More intense, frequent interaction becomes possible in small-group situations. But whether in small or large situations, children learn the give-and-take of communication as they share information and experiences. They learn to express ideas and opinions and to raise questions for further reflection. In this rhythm of intake of ideas and outgo of expression, teaching for depth learning is achieved.

PRACTICING SKILLS

Throughout a study children reveal the kinds of skills they need to learn and master. Alert teachers will pick up clues by observing what happens as children try to work toward their goals of study. As a class prepared for an election, their teacher noted that the children showed the need for skill in such matters as the following:

conducting a campaign for election;
securing pertinent information on problems arising;
spelling;
arranging poster materials;
using watercolor paints;
writing letters of invitation;
using parliamentary procedures in discussions.

By watching children during dramatic play, another teacher discovered their need for knowledge of how to:

use the telephone in taking orders and asking for information;
answer telephone questions accurately but briefly;
make change;
deal politely with customers;
record receipts.

Some of these skills belong to areas other than social studies, but there is no reason why a teacher should not pursue them at an appropriate time. Reference skills, map-globe skills, literacy skills, problem-solving skills, and skills of critical thinking all become essential tools for carrying through a unit-study.

Skills in interpersonal relations develop especially well as children work together toward group goals. Situations like the following demonstrate children's awareness and use of skills in working with other individuals.[2]

Ability to recognize the needs and rights of others—

Jim and Joe were talking about a mural they were painting. Jim pointed out that others in the room were trying to read and suggested they lower their voices.

[2]Examples are drawn from DeGraf Platte and others, "Skills in Human Relationships" (Mimeographed Report, California Association for Supervision and Curriculum Development, Southern Section Social Studies Committee, 1954).

Ability to control one's own feelings and predict consequences of own actions—

A committee was working on problems of houses. Alice and Helen wanted to read the same article during class time. Alice offered to take it home and read it that evening if Helen could finish it in class.

Ability to involve others and give everyone a sense of belonging—

The committee chairman noticed that all members except one had expressed ideas on the way in which the committee should report to the whole class. He asked that member if he would like to express his thoughts on the matter.

Skills in group procedures are closely related to skills of interpersonal relations. Here are examples of children's ability to handle skills in group procedures as they work with their peers:

Ability to use the techniques of problem solving—

Jane suggested to the class that the selection of questions for searching would run more smoothly if the class worked out a plan so that each member could have a turn to choose questions without having to argue.

Ability to master roles necessary to carry on group enterprises such as helping the group to clarify the problem and keep on the track—

In a discussion of the props to be used in dramatic play the group was planning, Jim reminded them they should decide on the background first, as the size of that would influence the size of props they could use.

Ability to maintain unpopular convictions without being offensive—

The class wanted some information on local health conditions and decided to send representatives to interview a local physician whom many of them knew. Ellen was the only class member who felt the health officer would be better able to give them the information needed. She volunteered to interview him after school and report to the class.

Ability to recognize special abilities needed for special jobs and select persons best qualified—

Ann suggested that Paul be chosen to interview the mayor because he always listened carefully and would be sure to report accurately to the class.

Whenever children show points of inadequacy in working as team members, the teacher will want to plan deliberately for direct attack upon the skills needed. Perhaps several days of short practice sessions over a period of weeks are needed, or perhaps only a single session. Practice may run concurrently with continued searches and organized activities.

The group had need to interpret graphic forms showing school growth, which the principal had loaned them. Several separate sessions during arithmetic periods were used to practice reading bars and graphs and learning how to prepare them.

Skills practice can be done as small group work.

Two of the boys especially able in handling wood construction work and equipment worked with one committee at a time to help them learn woodworking skills.

Skills practice may interrupt the ongoing work for a while.

The group discovered the need to practice alphabetizing names before they could complete their project of making a directory. They concentrated on this practice for several days before continuing with the directory.

Once children understand why they are practicing a skill, they can enter into the practice wholeheartedly to help themselves over the hurdle to action. When they accept the need for practice, they readily become involved in planning for it. The final test of mastery, however, is not in the practice of the skill but in its use. Only as the pupil uses the skill in action to help him achieve the goals of study, does the teacher discover his real level of skill efficiency.

REORGANIZING FOR ACTION

Taking continuous next steps during a study means further organization for action—new searches to make, new meanings to be clarified, goals to be evaluated and restated if necessary. At these times children reorient their thinking, extend their plans for action and reconsider the value of working with teams.

Reorienting children's thinking. Evaluation becomes necessary whenever children check to see what progress they are making and what purposes need to be redefined. This kind of evaluation, done as a continuous part of study, carries special momentum for renewed action. It occurs daily, not simply as a final culmination. Teachers help children to evaluate their situations with questions like these addressed to the group:

What do we need to do next in achieving our goals?
Are we satisfied now or do we need to go further into this?
Should we change our plans in light of what we now know?
Are we making progress toward our goals?

Such questions as these may be directed to individuals:

What do you hope to accomplish with this?
How can you correct what you're dissatisfied about?
How do you feel about what you've done?
What makes you think this is the best way to do it?

Children's complaints often imply the need for evaluation. Such remarks as "Do all of us need to do this?", "I need some help," "I don't think we're getting anywhere," and "Why should we do that?" become grounds for constructive group evaluation. As children gain strength in self-evaluation, they will raise their own standards for production and achievement. They will learn to use evaluation techniques to best advantage for reorienting their thinking and extending their plans for action.

Extending plans for action. Results of evaluation open up new needs for decisions and new needs for action. At times the teacher recognizes the need for new action.

During the reporting, the teacher noticed that children confused the leaders' places in time. She raised the possibility of making a large wall time-limit chart if it would help the group. Volunteers accepted the responsibility to work out this new plan of action.

At other times individual children take the initiative in arranging for new group action.

Discussions of sportsmanship led to the agreement that all would write a fictional but modern tale of sportsmanship. The results turned out to be so interesting to the group that someone suggested a book be made with them. A small committee offered to take on the editorial job.

Sometimes the entire class becomes almost spontaneously sparked with a need for action toward new goals.

The children only intended to satisfy their curiosity, but the results of their searching aroused the need for further action. Would it be possible to make an exhibit of their own to contribute to the exposition? They wondered. They wondered too if other children would be helped to understand the exposition better if they prepared a bulletin of their findings to distribute among the classrooms. The ideas were quickly accepted by the group and teacher, and new plans were laid to fulfill the new goals.

Some committees spark interest in common action:

The committee handling the physical education skills schedule presented its weekly plan to the group. The group evaluated it for balance and compared it with a month's plan. Interest was aroused in individual evaluation of physical skills. The committee agreed to prepare a form to be duplicated for individual use.

| Skill Chart | | | | Sharon Riley | |
Pitching	Batting	Kicking	Catching	Relays	Dates
bad	bad	bad	bad	pretty good	September 13
bad	bad	bad	bad	pretty good	September 20
bad	bad	bad	bad	pretty good	September 27
bad	bad	bad	improving	pretty good	October 4
improving	improving	improving	improving	pretty good	October 11
improving	improving	improving	improving	pretty good	October 18
approved by class	approved by class	approved by class	improving	pretty good	October 25

As plans are extended for further action, both teachers and pupils have the responsibility for recognizing the relationship between actions taken and the goals—old and new—to be achieved.

Using committee work. Some actions lend themselves to small group efforts better than others. However valuable committee work may be it does not constitute the total social studies program. Progress in a study does not always depend upon committee work. There are times when individuals work best alone or with a friend. There is no hard and fast rule relating to the use of committees. They should be used to the extent to which they enable individuals and groups to move toward their goals. If study after study, however, fails to make use of this procedure of learning, the values to be gained from close interpersonal relationships and group dynamics are lost. While some children achieve well, whether working alone or in groups, others find group work a definite stimulant to action. It is true, of course, that committee work sometimes results in uneven efforts and results—some members and some teams working more effectively than others. On the other hand, committee work often results in production superior to any one individual's efforts, not to mention that group work provides children with precious moments to expand and test out their thinking with others.

In any case the purpose of having children engage in small-group interactions goes deeper. By providing opportunity for learning mutual support and helpfulness, as well as allowing for interchange of talents and abilities, committee work places value upon individual differences used for a common purpose. This value is a basic premise of democratic living and a root of social learnings. With encouragement, committees learn to raise their standards of production and to profit from their mistakes.

At the teacher's suggestion, each committee prepared its "Standards for Committee Work." Each committee member kept a folder of his notes and drafts which he shared with committee members for corrections and suggestions.

Children learn how to choose their own committee members and chairman, or how to allow leadership to emerge as work progresses. Children unaccustomed to working as members of a group without close adult supervision and dictation may need special help in learning group process skills as well as independently handled research skills. In those cases the teacher takes a firmer hand in the group's make-up, himself choosing committee members and chairmen from volunteers. He works intensively with those individuals to help them gain strength both as group workers and as independent workers.

Committees vary in their purposes and children vary in their abilities to serve on different kinds of committees. It makes sense, then, for teachers to plan a wide range of committee activities. Some committees function as research teams, searching out information.

Each research team worked separately but reported back to the total group progress being made and needs yet to be met. As they did this, the teacher recorded on the chalkboard:

Date: March 10

Committee Chairman Reporting	Progress Reported	Needs Reported
Susan	2 reports almost ready	For information on the new aerospace industry
		To interview the superintendent on effects of new industry on school population

During progress reports other committees offered suggestions.

Some committees work as production teams.

The entire class agreed to build a bookstore to house original books by class authors. One committee served as construction workers, another as interior decorators, a third as publicity agents, a fourth as illustrators, a fifth as editors. Everyone was expected to try his hand at authorship, salesmanship, and readership.

Committees become planning-evaluating groups to stimulate the class or school to action goals.

The committee responsible for studying the effects of war upon Italian youth suggested in their report to the class that CARE packages be mailed as a way to help the young people. They also contacted each classroom in the school, explaining the project and enlisting further help. They arranged for publicity in the local newspaper and contacted the CARE office for information regarding procedures. After each weekly collection, they deposited the money in the local bank.

Committees need not all function at once, although they sometimes do. Depending upon its purpose, committee work alternates, some children working independently while others function in committees. At times only one committee works on a particular day or during a certain hour. With responsibilities clearly distributed, everyone can contribute to group effort in the ways he can best serve while, at the same time, the various jobs needed are carried on efficiently.

Whatever the next steps in reorganizing and resetting sights of committee work, care must be taken for action planned to move a study forward toward its goals of understandings and of action.

REACHING GOALS

What children do with their learnings falls naturally into line when teacher and pupils have determined the purposes of study and evaluated progress along the way. The goals themselves vary.

Solving a genuine problem. If a group has wrestled with a problem demanding realistic action, the goal is reached when the problem is solved. The problem may be concerned with improving the cafeteria situation, using time to personal and group advantage, conserving supplies, or resolving issues in class elections. Whether preparation for the solution requires a week's study or a month's, the study ends when action is taken to solve the problem. Questions such as "How shall we support the Red Cross this year?" "How shall we vote on the issue of lunchtime activities?" demand genuine decisions resulting in action. To act intelligently upon them requires study focused upon the problem. Not all goals of study need be problem-focused, but only problems genuine to children and capable of being solved by them should be so labeled.

Natural problem-solving situations occur throughout a study as obstacles to action arise and decisions are made to overcome them. Problems demanding solution face children in construction work, dramatization, preparations for interviews. Care should be taken to avoid contrived "problem" situations which are simply questions posed by the teacher. Acting out the teacher's question, "How did Daniel Boone feel in the wilderness?" may or may not arouse curiosity, but hardly constitutes a child's problem to be solved and acted upon by him. Likewise, studying the value of money because the teacher recognizes inefficient handling of allowances, may be useful, but cannot be considered a problem-solving experience if no problem-demanding action is felt by the children. Nor does studying mankind's problems or why people moved west create a problem-solving situation for children to act upon, although it does offer opportunity to analyze important situations. Before a study is justly labeled a problem-study, the teacher has these questions to consider:

Is the situation a genuine one upon which children will act?
Are there alternative paths of action which demand choices?
Does real action need to be taken as a result of study; that is, does the study hinge upon the solution to a conflict situation which the group recognizes and wishes to resolve?

For the major goal to be truly problem-centered, the answers should be in the affirmative.

Taking action upon a situation. If a group has conducted a study to prepare for an action project, the goal is reached when the project is launched. Action may be formal or informal; in either case there must be a real audience or beneficiaries, if the goal of study is to be counted as an action-oriented one

The group studied problems involved in the increase of population in their valley because they wished to submit to the chamber of commerce some information for its use. The completed report was not only sent to the chamber of commerce but published in the local newspaper. Writing a letter to the editor, the group publicly thanked participating citizens for their help:

PUPILS EXPRESS GRATITUDE
FOR POPULATION STUDY HELP

EDITOR: The fourth and fifth graders in Room __ at _____ School, wish to thank publicly the organizations and people who helped to answer questions regarding "Problems Involved in the Increase in Population in Our Valley."

Parents of all the boys and girls in Room __ who filled out questionnaires and helped to gather information also are thanked.

Many times after the results of searching are shared, groups plan "to do something" with their learnings. This is not the same as conducting a study *because* of action to be taken. Children studying toy shop workers sent toys they had constructed to needy children, but they had not set up their study for that purpose. On the other hand, the group which, having decided on a class breakfast, studied the social and economic as well as health aspects of breakfasts in order to assume proper responsibility for the action, set for themselves an action-oriented study. But having a waffle party or tacos dinner to "round out a study" does not make a study action-centered, whatever other values such an activity has.

Action of all kinds, of course, takes place during the conduct of a study. But only when the major action to be taken has become the goal of study should the study be labeled an action-study.

Coming to conclusions. If a group has decided to investigate a topic or a question or an issue which cannot be solved in an active sense by the group, conclusions drawn become the goal of study. Questions such as, Where should the new school be built? Why should the community have a swimming pool? Why have rules and regulations? Should there be only one newspaper in town? can be studied and recommendations made, but no real action can be taken to solve the problem.

Children studying poverty in South America drew conclusions like this:

One way of solving this problem of widespread poverty would be for us to send down people with scientific knowledge and new ideas and techniques for developing new industries and new ways of earning a living.

Intensive search for meanings usually precedes the drawing of conclusions. In studies of this kind, the conclusions drawn provide the satisfaction and take the place of elaborate culminating activities. The study is culminated when conclusions are reached.

Satisfying curiosities. An even simpler reason for study is high interest in "finding out." In these cases the goal is reached when curiosity is satisfied. Individualized studies especially lend themselves to such a goal.

Children pursuing the goal of satisfying their curiosities often want to make some tangible presentation of their findings to share with others. A mural, tape recording, original play, bulletin board display, class book, exhibit, model, quiz program—any of these activities which clarify meanings—also serves the purpose of sharing the results of curiosity.

Goals of study do not, of course, always fit neatly into one another. Overlapping of purposes occurs and dual purposes arise. Changes in plans shift the purpose of study so that new searchings and new clarifications of meanings are demanded. Whatever the case may be, both teacher and group should be clearly aware of their goals and able to justify their actions in terms of them.

Achieving goals of understanding. Whatever goals of the group are realized, the teacher's goals should remain in the background until he gains some insight into the kinds of understandings children have achieved as a result of study. Since formal testing is not likely to help a teacher do this, he needs to devise his own ways of discovery. He might ask the children to:

Record their opinions in response to a question.

To the question, What is your choice, the world of today, yesterday or tomorrow? there was this answer among others: "I like tomorrow because it's going to be different."

Write individual stories in relation to what they have learned.

The shoeshop man works hard. He works all day. He works for money. He works for his family.

Write individual stories in relation to what they have learned.

I didn't like learning it, but I learned that the United States doesn't practice what it preaches. The Negroes are persecuted in the South and elsewhere too. The hillbillies are made to live off by themselves in Chicago. Sammy Lee couldn't buy a house in Whittier, California.

There are signs in Los Angeles saying "Gentiles Only." I think the United States should clean its own house before it starts telling the rest of the world how to live.

Illustrate a term wherein children give their individual version before a study and again after the study has been completed.

Before a study of Pioneer Life	*After a study of Pioneer Life*
settlers with guns (John)	Ross discovering ice shelf in Antarctica (John)
covered wagons (Mary)	bathyscoping (Mary)
fighting Indians (Tom)	heart machine in action (Tom)
chopping wood to build cabins (Joe)	jet flights (Joe)
cactus land (Henry)	the world of Africa (Henry)
buckskin-dressed men (Jane)	spaceship to "who knows where" (Jane)

List conclusions as a group.

We should remember there are other religions in the world besides our own.

We should respect other people's religion and try to understand why people believe as they do.

We should be proud and not ashamed of our own religion.

Record evaluations individually.

Prejudice is an awful word. To me it means some opinion or feeling not based on facts, for or against something

Evaluate the processes used.

It's a nice feeling being independent of any social studies book with big black print. I think it is more interesting to go to the library and hunt for information than it is having it right in front of your eyes. I think that as far as the information goes, we learn just about three times as much as we learn regularly and we remember it. There are some bad points, like going to the library asking for an article on Khrushchev and being told, "We have nothing on Khrushchev in the children's section."

List group learnings.

We learned about different languages and learned to say a few words in other languages.

We learned how language was long ago and how it is now.

We learned that words have different meanings for different people.

We learned how words were made up—sounds, root words, suffixes, and prefixes.

We learned that people from other countries have their words and we have ours. But when we get together we find that they have some of of ours and we have some of theirs.

Teachers themselves observe evidence of understandings achieved when children talk and act, as did the teacher recording these comments.

Skippy now can't stand a bit of unfairness and he was once notorious for unfair play.

Susan invited the new girl to pitch, saying to me, "She needs a chance."

The team captain gives girls a chance now and encourages them to continue playing when they lose courage.

Alvin made the comment, "She has to practice some more," instead of his more usual destructive kind.

Mary announced that her father was helping her to practice pitching balls. She said he hadn't realized it was so important to her.

There are other ways too—conducting interviews with individuals and small groups, analyzing informal test situations, planning role-playing sessions—the same ways a teacher uses to uncover clues for teaching.

Many times teachers discover what children have gained, not at the "end" of a study but months or years later as they observe them in new situations. In this sense studies do not end but continue to show results in reflections and behaviors whenever children talk and act.

Throughout a study and long after, the teacher continually evaluates for himself what children have achieved. If his evaluation is a favorable one, he has the right to feel that he too has reached a goal. He has the right to feel satisfaction in knowing that he has helped children as they solve problems, take actions, draw conclusions, and explore curiosities—grow toward understanding through social studies.

Chapter IV

ACHIEVING A UNIT-STUDY APPROACH

Studies based on significant understandings have certain desirable characteristics for the teacher to recognize in his own planning and evaluation. First, of course, is the *unity* of study which is achieved when goals of understanding have been sharply defined and pinpointed as a focus of activity. Second, is the *shared responsibility* achieved when children are consulted in setting up purposes for study and in planning the means to meet the purposes. Third, is the *integration* of effort which is achieved as searches for information are organized and reorganized, material-sources gathered, meanings clarified, and action taken to fulfill the goals of study. Fourth, adequate *timing* for study-action is achieved when the focus remains on study goals, not time schedules. Fifth, *balance* within a study and among studies is achieved by careful planning and record-keeping.

Teachers who use a unit-study approach in teaching social studies will want to rethink the meaning of these characteristics in terms of classroom action.

Unit of Study

Thinking through significant understandings is a major task for the teacher. Thinking through learning activities which will promote most directly and efficiently children's growth toward the understandings is another major task, sometimes more difficult than the first. To select learning activities in relation to the selected understandings requires screening out irrelevant activities, no matter how "interesting" they seem to be.

PRE-PLANNING

For the teacher who wishes to see at a glance whether the study planned with children has unity, whether the learning activities suggested relate directly and efficiently to the understandings to be achieved and problems and questions to be tackled, work sheets like these help:

Goal of Understanding:

To see the relationship between public schools and the goals of our democracy.

Understandings	Topics	Learning Activities
Public schools reflect our democratic beliefs and goals and work toward achieving them:	Why we have American Education Week	Discuss American Education Week
	What our schools teach and why	Plan play for P-TA
—effective functioning of a democratic society requires that each individual be provided with full educational opportunity	What we get out of school	Read history of education
	Growth of our public school system	Talk with parents, grandparents, older neighbors
—in our society the public schools belong to all the people and depend upon their understanding and support.	Work of Horace Mann and other leaders	Prepare biographies of leaders
	Purpose of school boards	Attend schoolboard meeting

Whatever form they take, work sheets are merely rough drafts of plans made and remade with pupil consultation. This kind of planning eliminates elaborate listing of general objectives and skills which belong to almost every study undertaken. It avoids, too, the random listing of activities and long lists of book and film titles which too easily become outdated. There are innumerable resource units available on the market, not to mention college-type textbooks and local publications filled with lists of general objectives, skills, activities and materials. Any of these can be scanned by the teacher as an aid to his own planning. There is no need for the teacher to duplicate them.

Working with Goals of Understanding

Within children's backgrounds of ability to understand, almost any understanding may be developed. But how deeply will depend, of course, upon the group's skill in handling the big idea in specific terms. This the teacher must judge.

Children may or may not be aware of the goals of understanding as such. In any case they will formulate their own generalizations from the specifics which they have absorbed. They must be free to formulate them in their own way if empty verbalizations are to be avoided. The teacher's role remains one of stimulating impressions and encouraging expressions. He maintains responsibility not only for selecting appropriate goals of understanding, but also for judging the most effective ways to teach toward their realization. Certainly, working with goals of understanding is not a matter of handing out generalizations for children to illustrate. Such goals are simply the teacher's directional points. They serve best as focus for building concrete experiences.

Choosing a Focus

Within any topic there are innumerable avenues of pursuit. For example, in the area of identifying with others there are these possibilities for understanding family life and one's own growing up.

FOR PRIMARY GRADES

Pertaining to Family Life and Other People

Learning in the Family	Family Routines
Family Interests	Going Places with Our Family
Building a New House	Families on the Move
What Makes a Family?	Home in a Trailer Court
Helping at Home	Families We Know
Storybook Families	Family Friends
Services in the Home	People We Meet and Talk with
Changing Family Roles	Everyday
Languages Around the World	Rural Living

Pertaining to Ourselves

How We Spend Our Time	It's Fun to Have Friends

Choosing Free-Time Activities
Planning Summer Activities
Ways We Learn
Watching TV
Getting to Know Ourselves
    Better
Staying Healthy
Our Feelings
Getting Along with Others
Our Belongings
Camping
Children's Rights and
    Responsibilities
How Do We Work as a Group?

Sharing with Others
What Does It Mean to
    Communicate?
Reading on My Own
What's Coming in the Future?
Meals Around the Clock
Groups to Join
Becoming a Cub Scout, Brownie,
    Bluebird
Participating in a Drive, e.g.,
    Junior Red Cross, Toys for
    Children's Hospital, Neighbor-
    hood Clean Up
Using What I Have Learned

FOR INTERMEDIATE GRADES

Pertaining to Family Life and Other People

Family Customs and Traditions
Family Travels
Families on the Move
Family Activities
How Families Earn Their Living
Using Money in the Family
How Science Has Changed Fam-
    ily Living

Family Plans for the Future
Families Come West
Why Have Families?
Family Influences
Planning a Party
People We Know
Friends and Others
Language as Communication

Pertaining to Ourselves

Solving Group Problems
Why We Join Groups
People We Admire
Growing Up
Using Our Feelings
How We Use Our Time
The Job I Would Like to Have
What Makes Us Tick?

When I Grow Up
Making Up Our Minds
Other People's Beliefs
Planning Time for Voluntary Ac-
    tivities
Planning Summer Activities
Joining a Club
Making Friends
Power of Words

Obviously some focus is needed, but what that focus should be depends upon the understandings to be emphasized. Take, for example, a study revolving around the usefulness of automobiles to people. If the focus were drawn from the area of choosing goods and services, the goal of understanding might be: taking into account factors involved in the choice and use of goods and services. The general understanding here could be that the economic welfare of the individual and that of the group are interrelated. In this case the study would probably spotlight the relationship between employment in the automobile industry and people's choices and uses of automobiles.

If the focus were drawn instead from the area of participating in the world of work, the goal of understanding might be: recognizing the value of all work. In this case the general understanding could be that many different kinds of work are necessary to keep a modern society operating. The study itself could spotlight the workers involved in both wholesale and retail service and repair divisions of the automobile business; or those engaged in road-building.

If the focus were drawn from the area of using time, the goal of understanding could be: realizing that people will have an increasing amount of time free from work demands. Here the general understanding would be that the trend toward more free time is increasing fastest in the more highly industrialized countries. The study might revolve around such topics as automobile travel in vacation time, comparisons of modes of travel, including historical comparisons, and/or comparisons among developed and undeveloped nations.

There may be occasions when the goal of understanding is vague; when children simply explore the scope of an area or a broad topic. Generally speaking, however, studies entitled "Mexico," "Civil War," "Community Living," "Home and Family," "Our State, Past and Present," "The Dairy," and similar studies have no intrinsic focus. Because almost everything falls within their scope, such topics provide no guidelines for unit development. They give no safeguards against superficial, sweeping coverage or the use of trite procedures.

SHARED RESPONSIBILITY

The teacher's planning in no way substitutes for teacher–pupil planning. The teacher and pupils working together develop and clarify the purposes for each study and commit themselves to action. Jointly they indicate study topics, suggest questions to guide and direct the study's development. They plan together those experiences which in their judgment will best achieve their purposes and which, at least in the teacher's mind, will lead to a deepening understanding of big ideas.

DELEGATION OF RESPONSIBILITY

Delegation of responsibility, if needed, might be charted in this way:

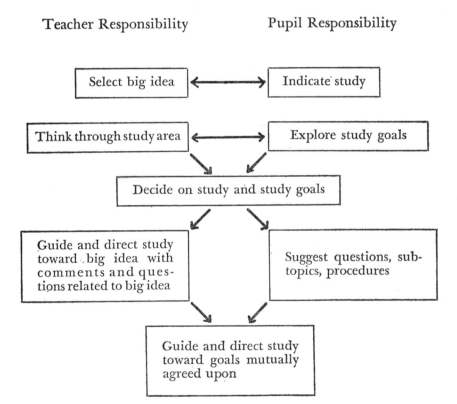

Teacher Responsibility   Pupil Responsibility

Select big idea ⟷ Indicate study

Think through study area ⟷ Explore study goals

Decide on study and study goals

Guide and direct study toward big idea with comments and questions related to big idea

Suggest questions, subtopics, procedures

Guide and direct study toward goals mutually agreed upon

In spite of delegated responsibility, the lines shift and flow with particular teacher and group abilities. In no case should the teacher's planning crowd out children's chances to participate on as many levels of planning as they can. For unless a study emerges *with* the group in a total sense, there is no true experience of co-operative study in progress.

GENUINE CHOICE MAKING

To propose a topic to children and then invite them to suggest subtopics with the question, What would you like to find out about this topic? too often leads to repetitive thinking. Year after year children identify the familiar subtopics of food, clothing, shelter, transportation. When pupils repeatedly have no choice of major study but limitless choice of subtopics, practice in deep, significant probings is lost in routine, stereotyped thinking. As such a habit becomes ingrained, children find it increasingly difficult to identify genuine, specific problems and exciting controversies which affect them and all mankind.

Studies following textbook units not only fall short of focus, but seriously restrict choice-making. With the subject and pages fixed, there is even less opportunity to plan a unit-study in relation to children's questions and problems and critical thought. While the reading of a textbook page or a chapter, as in the case of broad area studies, may lead to curiosities which launch a unit-study, neither type of experience in itself fulfills the requirements of a unit-study approach to learning.

Planning a study with children on the basis of goals of understanding requires the teacher to exercise marked self-discipline. Not just any study will do. Not just any procedures will suffice. Planning with children assumes that the teacher has faith in children's ability to become fully participating members in group decision-making experiences. It assumes that the teacher feels deep conviction regarding the importance of the understandings to be developed. Understandings become urgent goals to achieve and the core of unit-study planning.

Integration of Study

Integration of study occurs through the interrelationship of subject matter content, feeling content, and skill content. In an integrated study children not only gain a sense of the interrelationships in subject matter and among subjects, but learn to respect all kinds of content as useful tools to unified thinking, feeling, and acting.

INTEGRATION OF SKILL CONTENT

Certain skills outside the scope of social studies become necessary to move a study forward.

Language skills. While all studies make use of language to communicate ideas, the kinds of language skills used vary with intent. Language activities may be limited to reading and recitation, with occasional report-writing and use of the dictionary and encyclopedia. Or language activities may be greatly broadened to include informal conversations, formal discussions, buzz-group interactions, tape recording, speech-making, role-playing. They may include note-taking, writing captions, stories, letters, plays, movies. Naturally, the broader the range of language experiences planned, the more likelihood of deeper and richer learning results for children.

Social skills. Social skills, too, become an integral part of study, the more so when the conduct of the study is planned deliberately to use them. As children work together, they have opportunity to learn the dynamics of small- and large-group action; to learn good feelings toward themselves and others; and to use social skills for increased productivity of ideas and expressions. Social skills include:

giving, interpreting, and listening to suggestions;
raising questions for the group to consider;
stating alternatives clearly before the group;
deciding when to delegate tasks to a committee;
choosing people best qualified for particular jobs;
estimating people and materials needed for the job;
planning work to make best use of individual abilities;
talking over plans with other committee members;
presenting steps for action to the group;
deciding what to do when a plan fails;
using records as guides to group action;
explaining reasons for disagreements;
fulfilling commitments accepted;
using courteous language and gestures;

knowing names of fellow group members;
serving as group leader.

These and others become essential to a study designed to make full use of social skills.

Art and other skills. Other skill areas also provide tools for communication and expression of social studies learnings. As children have opportunity to draw, paint, or represent their ideas in clay to clarify their thinking in relation to the questions at hand; as they cut, paste, sculpture, and print the results of their searches to share with others, they use art as an integral part of study. Children use varied musical skills when they create songs and dances to express themselves, to clarify meanings, or to reach goals of understanding. They use varied arithmetical skills when they apply numbers to the solution of problems or the achievement of goals. In this sense there is no limit to the scope of skills which may be involved in a unit-study.

INTEGRATION OF SUBJECT-MATTER CONTENT

Varied subject-matter content as well as skill content is used in an integrated study. To answer the question, Why do we have zoos? might require an understanding of wild animal habitats. Such a science emphasis becomes necessary to the progress of the study. A study focused upon toyshop workers may demand an understanding of how workers put toys together. Scientific information concerning operational features of toys again becomes essential to the conduct of the study. Children engaged in the goal of preparing a breakfast learn health aspects of breakfasting. In short, as content from fields other than the social sciences becomes *essential* to the pursuit of intelligent study and understanding of socially based meanings, an integrated relationship is established.

INTEGRATION, NOT CORRELATION

Integrated activities should not be confused with correlated activities. Many times content and activities show correlation but not integration. A study focused upon work at the airport does not necessarily call for an understanding of what makes airplanes fly. This may be an interest of the group but, if so, becomes a correlated science interest, not an integral part of the study. A study which concentrates upon the pioneer movement in America would not require knowledge of astronomy and star navigation to understand the social aspects. Although such a science study might be interesting, using a far-fetched science topic to complement a social studies unit-study does not result in a unified study. Neither do activities carried on as "enrichment."

Learning the song "Little Red Caboose," and reading a story of *The Little Engine That Could* in relation to a study involving freight train services may be enriching experiences. Molding clay objects or creating arithmetic problems using "a visit to Mexico" as the story background in relation to a study of the Mexican culture may likewise be worth-while experiences. Such activities correlate with the study but may not be integrated. Only when the activity and the content are required to search out information and clarify meanings in relation to the goals of study do they function in an integrated manner.

While children may be keenly interested in correlated materials, teachers should not take it for granted that they are. Children can be absorbed in the main topic, yet disinterested in the correlated materials offered. Although correlation has value perhaps in enjoyment and interest, the conduct of study focused upon particular social understandings is not dependent upon correlated material. False relationships are set up when correlated activities are used with the assumption that they are necessary to the study. With care, teachers can concentrate upon building integrated studies which serve the cause of both unity and economy.

Timing the Study

Whatever time it takes to examine, compare, and build meanings is the time which should be planned for a unit-study. Some studies last merely days or a week or two; others need months of investigation. Time limits are best set by the group as the members decide what tasks are to be accomplished and what goals are to be met. There is no glory in simply covering ground. "Covering" material within arbitrary time limits too often means hasty teaching and superficial learning. Expressed by the artist Morandi: "To achieve understanding it is necessary not to see many things but to look hard at what you do see." Timing in this sense becomes important.

Balance of Study

However deep children must look to gain insight, they need also, for adequate living in today's and tomorrow's world, to be practiced in handling varied kinds of understandings, skills, and behaviors. To achieve balance requires long-term planning in which teachers look backward as well as forward.

Long-Term Planning

The studies themselves suggest the need for balance. Because not all studies are designed to achieve the same purposes, children will benefit from dealing with varied goals, ranging from satisfaction of curiosity to drawing conclusions or solving problems. Children will profit from delving into differing areas of focus, ranging from studies identified with aspects of personal living to those concerned with world affairs or local and historical actions. Children will also gain from learning to adapt procedures of working to particular goals of study, with activities ranging from dramatization or committee research to independent reading and original searching.

There can be no hard and fast rule to alternating kinds of studies and kinds of learning activities. Sometimes a "doubletake," that is, following one study with another of similar emphasis, is needed to develop a certain understanding. Or special needs occur for emphasizing a certain understanding over a period of several years. Particular groups of children need emphasis upon certain skills, understandings and procedures. It is the long-term view which counts.

The teacher who wishes to develop as balanced a program as possible will, of necessity, learn what other teachers have tried to accomplish. He will gladly participate as a staff team-member in planning adequate programs. A faculty working together can think through possible studies which would have current social significance. They may choose to work on common understandings identified in different ways by different groups of children. They may choose to divide certain understandings according to their own interests and strengths, and the interests and strengths of their groups. They may discuss what they have learned about their group's needs and abilities, and share their plans for meeting their particular situations. All this becomes long-term planning for a balanced program.

RECORD-KEEPING

Records which show children's actual accomplishments and teachers' actual intentions open the way toward achieving true balance. Records of experiences kept by each teacher enable succeeding teachers to extend and refine previous learnings and to move toward new possibilities for study. In this sense, records become an essential part of planning. They need not be elaborate. The work sheets used for planning, with proper revisions as plans change, serve as simple records to use for future reference. Or a form of this kind suffices:

Inventory of Experiences

Grade	Teacher	Year

Please record briefly what you did to help children increase their understandings in social studies:

Area of Experience: Dates
1. Understandings emphasized:
   General
   Specific
2. Unit-study title:
3. Major problems, questions, or topics attacked:
4. Major learning activities:
5. Major sources of information used:

Recording only unit titles becomes meaningless as a guide to future planning. Such titles as "Zoo," "Pioneers," with no further information to explain them, leave a false impression of coverage and no knowledge of the emphases. Relying upon curriculum guides for assuming children's past experiences also builds false security; for it reveals neither what children absorbed nor what the teacher emphasized. To use them as records for scope and sequence is to ignore the nature of learning. True scope and sequence of programs grow as teachers take time to plan *with* children and learn for themselves what children have absorbed and what they demonstrate as their understandings.

KINDS OF BALANCE

As teachers plan on the basis of children's previous experiences and learnings, they will maintain many kinds of balance:

Balance between and among studies. For working toward understanding is a long-term program.

Balance between skills and subject matter content. For both skills and subject matter are tools for learning.

Balance between study and action. For results of searching must penetrate to the roots of being.

Balance between depth and breadth. For new vistas of thinking must be opened up while older ones are developed more thoroughly.

Balance between planning and evaluating. For next steps need always to be indicated.

Teachers who feel confident and responsible for using their own intelligence and creativeness will find innumerable ways to build a balanced program of social studies for children. They will find the courage to rethink the unit approach in order to rebuild its vitality.

Valuing the Unit-Study

Well-designed and productively used, the unit-study offers children the challenge and excitement of thinking through problems, making decisions and being able to act upon them. It gives both purpose and practice to the many skills of group and individual living. There is self-discipline involved in learning to hold steadfast to goals and to weed out efforts and interests extraneous to the purposes to which individuals and groups become committed. At the same time there is need for individual talents and gifts, as children pursue individual tasks within the framework of common concerns.

When the unit-study originates and unfolds as a genuine concern of the group in the area of human interaction, it becomes a teacher's valuable resource for helping children reach understandings through social studies. Man lives on hope. Today's children are tomorrow's hope.

4-160

192